SELECTED POEMS OF

JOHN CLARE

THE POETRY BOOKSHELF

General Editor: James Reeves

Robert Graves: *English and Scottish Ballads*
Tom Scott: *Late Medieval Scots Poetry*
James Reeves: *Chaucer: Lyric and Allegory*
William Tydeman: *English Poetry 1400–1580*
Martin Seymour-Smith: *Shakespeare's Sonnets*
Martin Seymour-Smith: *Longer Elizabethan Poems*
James Reeves: *John Donne*
Jack Dalglish: *Eight Metaphysical Poets*
James Reeves and Martin Seymour-Smith: *Andrew Marvell*
Gareth Reeves: *George Herbert*
Dennis Burden: *Shorter Poems of John Milton*
V. de S. Pinto: *Poetry of the Restoration*
Roger Sharrock: *John Dryden*
John Heath-Stubbs: *Alexander Pope*
Francis Venables: *The Early Augustans*
Donald Davie: *The Late Augustans*
F. W. Bateson: *William Blake*
G. S. Fraser: *Robert Burns*
Roger Sharrock: *William Wordsworth*
James Reeves: *S. T. Coleridge*
Robin Skelton: *Lord Byron*
John Holloway: *P. B. Shelley*
James Reeves: *John Clare*
Robert Gittings: *Poems and Letters of John Keats*
Edmund Blunden: *Alfred Lord Tennyson*
James Reeves: *Robert Browning*
Denys Thompson: *Poetry and Prose of Matthew Arnold*
James Reeves: *Emily Dickinson*
James Reeves: *G. M. Hopkins*
David Wright: *Seven Victorian Poets*
James Reeves: *The Modern Poets' World*
James Reeves: *D. H. Lawrence*

SELECTED POEMS OF
JOHN CLARE

Edited with an Introduction

by

JAMES REEVES

HEINEMANN

LONDON

Heinemann Educational Books Ltd

LONDON EDINBURGH MELBOURNE AUCKLAND TORONTO
HONG KONG SINGAPORE KUALA LUMPUR NEW DELHI
NAIROBI JOHANNESBURG LUSAKA IBADAN
KINGSTON

ISBN 0 435 15005 7

FIRST PUBLISHED 1954

REPRINTED 1961, 1964, 1966, 1968, 1969,
1973, 1976, 1978

JOHN CLARE

1793–1864

Published by
Heinemann Educational Books Ltd
48 Charles Street, London W1X 8AH
Printed and bound in Great Britain by
Morrison & Gibb Ltd, London and Edinburgh

CONTENTS

The text of these poems, and their chronological arrangement, are taken from Professor J. W. Tibble's two volume edition (Dent, 1935)

INTRODUCTION

I

READERS of anthologies may find it difficult to appreciate the poems of Clare. They do not appear at their best in small quantities. The most satisfactory anthology poem is short, vivid, technically competent, striking, or even dramatic. Clare wrote few poems of this kind. His thought is often slight, his imagery delicately coloured, he is seldom, if ever, dramatic; his voice is not easily heard amidst a clamour. Some of his best poems are long and, from a formal point of view, ill constructed; worst of all, he has faults of diction and grammar which the reader must simply ignore. Clare was one of the most poorly educated of all great poets; much of his work was corrected by editors and friends; but there remain errors of style, especially that of repetition, which might easily have been corrected. Very few poems are without technical blemishes. If one reads Clare's poems in bulk, one can get used to these blemishes, ignore them, or even come to love them, though one may continue to fear that they may put off other readers. For the faults are part of the poems and the poems are the expression of the man. Clare never achieved perfect technical competence, but he had, as it were from birth, what is much rarer and more valuable—natural taste, craftsmanship, and poetic integrity. Though the style may at times be clumsy and awkward, we feel that the mind of the writer is essentially refined; the craftsmanship is sound, though sometimes rough; the poet's integrity immunised Clare against the temptation to be pretentious or insincere. This integrity was protected by a certain stubborn independence. Whatever Clare did not know as a literary man, he felt that he knew his business as a poet. He knew, for instance, that, however high his gifts might raise him above the mental level of his own people and their narrow range of sensibility, it was their speech which was the basic material of his poems. His fame gained him the friendship of Charles Lamb, which he prized dearly; Lamb was a critic of high reputation. When he advised Clare, however, to use fewer rustic expressions, Clare quietly—and rightly—ignored the advice. There are occasions when he lapsed into the artificial poetic language of the eighteenth century, but these grew rarer as he developed; and in the main his language is firmly based in the unaffected speech of his native country-side. Clare was not an anthology poet. His qualities are not epitomised in brief, quotable lyrics. His poems are like the central English country-side where they grew, unsensational, undramatic, revealing their beauties more to the dweller than to the visitor. The qualities of such scenery are secret and intimate. Yet the poems need selection. The landscape has dull stretches, patches of repetition, and occasional intrusions by non-native elements. Clare was not good at drinking songs, for instance, or pastiche folk-ballads. This selection contains enough to give a full account of Clare's genius, and to show him throughout the range of his work, from the earliest to the latest, from the most simply descriptive to the most profoundly reflective, from the height of rapture to the depth of utter despair. The reader who wishes for a smaller sample of the poems might begin with the following:

Autumn ('Siren of sullen moods . . . ', p. 38); *Summer Images* (p. 42); *The Eternity of Nature* (p. 43); *Song's Eternity* (p. 80); *Break of Day* (p. 101); *Gipsies* (p. 102); *The Exile* (p. 104); *Autumn* ('The thistledown's flying . . . ', p. 114); *Clock-a-clay* (p. 123); *The Dying Child* (p. 124); *First Love* ('I never was struck . . . ', p. 128); *Secret Love* (p. 129); *Invitation to Eternity* (p. 130); *Poets Love Nature* (p. 131); *I Am* (p. 132).

In these fifteen poems the unfamiliar reader may find the soul of Clare: its untroubled delight in the humblest manifestations of nature; its desire for ideal love; its high concern for poetry; its terrible bewilderment and dismay at what life can do to it. There is enough to persuade the most demanding reader that Clare's poetry is worth further exploration.

II

'I loved nature & painted her both in words & colours better than many Poets & Painters . . . in my boyhood Solitude was the most talkative vision I met with Birds bees trees flowers all talked to me incessantly louder than the busy hum of men. . . .' (*From a letter to his son, Charles Clare, from Northampton Asylum*, 1848.)

THE expression 'nature-lover' suggests nowadays a week-end rambler, a keen gardener, perhaps even an amateur naturalist. Since the Wordsworthian revolution English people have increasingly prided themselves on being nature-lovers, and increasingly lived in towns. This is not inconsistent if we read 'nature-lover' in a special sense, as one who loves nature not because he lives with her but because he has lost her. This is not the sense in which Clare was a nature lover and in which the greater part of his poems are nature poems.

Clare did not, of course, invent nature poetry. He was not the first poet who lived and worked in the fields. But nature has a place in his poetry which it had not in that of any other poet before or since. It is the mark of a lover, in the purest sense, that he can, at least temporarily, lose his identity in the contemplation of the object of his love. This happened to Clare habitually, for long stretches of time, and with apparent effortlessness. It did not happen with Burns or Thompson before him, and it could scarcely happen to any poet in the urban age which followed.

This apparent objectivity in Clare's poems occurs again and again. It is indeed their normal habit. One might read pages and pages of Clare's poems and suppose them to be 'merely descriptive.' If this happens, one is deceived.

There is a type of skilled journalism or reporting which can be called merely descriptive and is sometimes praised for its objectivity. But there is no virtue in objectivity for its own sake; photography is an art only by virtue of the subtle exploitation of the possibilities of lighting and composition.

For Clare, objectivity was a method, not an end. The commonest expression in all his nature poetry is 'I love'— often extended to 'I love to hear' or 'I love to see.' The expression is used sometimes as a formal opening to a descriptive poem; even when it is omitted, the sense of it is always there. Clare's minute observation, his lingering over the details of a country scene, his intense interest in the plainest and most homely manifestations of life on the land, could arise only from a disinterested and self-forgetful love. He loses himself in nature, it surrounds him; he is not a visitor among the fields, he does not look at the country-side from the snug cosiness of a window-seat. We should know this from his poems, even if we knew nothing of his life.

His attitude to the country neighbours who appear throughout his poems is the same. He loves them, yet he stands apart —not out of condescension or superiority, but from the plain fact that a poet, however much he is part of the society in which he is born and lives, is set apart from it by his gifts. He can, like any other villager with some sensibility, sentimentalise over a pretty milkmaid or mock at a loutish barbarian. He writes of cottage life with a sort of detached love, a shy intimacy.

To enjoy Clare's naturalistic poetry more or less free from reflection or subjective emotion, read *The Maple-tree* (p. 123), *A Hill-side House* (p. 99), and *Grasshopper* (p. 92). Poems a little more atmospheric, a little more subtly *composed*, are *The Silver Mist* (p. 117), *The Autumn Wind* (p. 115), *Winter Weather* (p. 101), *Deluge* (p. 101), and *The Breath of Morning* (p. 67). *Insects* (p. 47) is a poem which expresses love with perfect appropriateness and the most joyful simplicity of feeling.

Clare loved not only nature but poetry as well. These two loves awoke together in his heart as a boy, and never left him. It would be wrong to present him as a naïve countryman, 'the idle singer of an empty day,' pouring out artless ditties like a nightingale. He was always a conscious craftsman. As has been said, he never achieved a slick fluency, fluent though he was. We feel that as a rule his ear and his vocabulary were adequate and no more than adequate. But beneath his artlessness there is hidden more art than perhaps he has been given credit for. It did not take him long to realise that polite diction was out of place. 'Blooming,' 'pleasing,' 'Say, maiden,' 'the smile of plenty,' and 'envy's sneer' are expressions that occur in what are on the whole good poems. But for the most part the reader must accept such blemishes and note that they became fewer as Clare's poetry progressed. What is more remarkable, though less obvious, is his naturalness in verse. He managed to write long, regularly rhymed poems with scarcely any inversions, scarcely even any deviations from the language of ordinary conversation. He was generally content with an established metrical form, usually a simple one, but he never ceased to try experiments, often evolving a metrical variation of great charm. The beautiful five-line stanza of *The Dying Child* is a rare innovation ; so, too, is the light and airy texture of *Break of Day*.

So far, then, from being ever 'merely descriptive' or naturalistic, Clare habitually cultivated his double love in the care which he bestowed on the selection and arrangement of his impressions. He wrote too much and pruned too little. But why not? The immense bulk of his output is proof of his devotion to poetry. He wrote because he could not help it. After he was about thirty he had very little critical help, and his poems were not prepared for publication. There is in existence a mass of material which he probably would not have wished to publish. He cannot be censured for the profusion of his output nor, in the circumstances, for the inequality of its worth. We must judge him by the considerable bulk of poems of remarkable quality and by those few which transcend the general level and may be fairly placed with the best English poems of all times.

III

BEFORE going further, I shall make some detailed comments on a single nature poem, choosing for this purpose one of the sonnets of the middle period. *Summer Moods* is no more than an average poem, no better and no worse than dozens of others. It is taken as characteristic of the general level of the shorter nature poems. It is simply the expression of a mood that was often with Clare, not the result of the sudden excitement that comes to a poet when he has something special to say. That is one of the astonishing things about Clare: he was the absolute opposite of an *occasional* poet. Not that he did not, or could not, turn out occasional poems. No one was ever more continuously and unremittingly a poet. It seems that even in the depths of despair and depression his rhyming faculty never left him for long. *Summer Moods*, then, is just one of his everyday things.

SUMMER MOODS

I love at eventide to walk alone,
   Down narrow lanes o'erhung with dewy thorn,
Where from the long grass underneath, the snail
   Jet-black creeps out and sprouts his timid horn.
I love to muse o'er meadows newly mown,
   Where withering grass perfumes the sultry air,
Where bees search round with sad and weary drone
   In vain for flowers that bloomed but newly there;
While in the juicy corn, the hidden quail
   Cries 'Wet my foot!' and, hid as thoughts unborn,
The fairy-like and seldom seen land-rail
   Utters 'Craik, craik,' like voices underground.
Right glad to meet the evening's dewy veil,
   And see the light fade into glooms around.

The faults are of the kind usual with Clare. They are obvious and pardonable. The repetition of 'newly,' the juxtaposition of 'hidden' and 'hid,' and the faulty grammatical connection, of the last two lines are weaknesses which indicate no general feebleness of conception or execution. The rhythmic awkwardness of the line about the 'land-rail' is perhaps not a fault. But nothing can take from the authenticity of the experience. The mood of a summer evening is unmistakably suggested, with sureness of touch and delicacy of observation. In the first four lines the mind's eye moves down the thorn-crowned hedge to focus on the tiny black snail beneath it, creeping out to enjoy the damp safety of twilight. In the second four lines there is an appeal to the sense of smell, and once more the focus of the scene is a small creature, the droning bee searching wearily for the flowers which have been cut down with the grass. The reader's ear, aroused by the sound of the bee, is ready to respond to the onomatopoeic renderings of the cries of quail and land-rail, invisible in the fields. Once more the reader's eye is appealed to, and in the final two lines the whole scene is dissolved in twilight. But the poem is not merely the re-creation of a sensuous experience. There is emotion also, quiet, subdued, 'hid as thoughts unborn,' an undercurrent of feeling like the 'underground' voice of the land-rail.[1] The repeated 'I love' is no empty phrase. In the adjectives 'timid,' 'sad and weary' there is the hint of a profound sympathy with the small creatures of the fields. This tenderness of feeling pervades all Clare's nature poems. It cannot be faked. It is too constant, too spontaneous, too organically interwoven in the substance of all Clare's writing to be mistaken for anything but the core and centre of the poet's being.

The existence of Clare the poet is, of course, a miracle. It is not miraculous that a country labourer should have felt profoundly about the country-side. Many are oblivious to their surroundings, but many are innately responsive. The miracle is that a man of such tender sensibility should have been so continuously articulate, and possessed of the natural taste never to stray for long outside his true poetic milieu. If Clare 'knew his place' poetically, it was not through any grovelling sense of social submission; it was through his natural artistic integrity which protected him like a charm.

There is a sense of organic harmony between poet and nature discoverable in the bulk of Clare's work. This is its most precious gift. Clare was a happy poet; there is more happiness in his poetry than in that of most others. This was no mere animal contentment of body and senses, but a quiet ecstasy and inward rapture. Such happiness is not to be had except at a price.

IV

CLARE'S poems have been considered so far without reference to his life. Such few facts as have been mentioned could be

[1] That this bird had a special significance for Clare, and is mentioned by no mere accident of poetic fancy, is shown by the following remark in a letter to Hessey, Taylor's partner, in 1823: ' . . . The landrail or landrake . . . a little thing heard about the grass & wheat in summer & one of the most poetical images in rural nature tis like a spirit you may track it by its noise a whole day & never urge it to take wing.'

deduced from his work. Too much attention has been focused on his life, and too much vicarious sympathy expended on a poet dead for nearly a century by those who would be as little help to him, were he living, as the mass of his contemporaries were. One way to show sincere pity for the fate of Clare is to take an interest in his living descendants, the poets of to-day. After his triumph as a young man, Clare suffered gradual neglect and starvation. Nowadays we should not starve him, we should find a job for him in some bureaucratic organisation—a much surer way to stifle his poetic spirit. For the protective folds of a modern corporation may be a more effective prison than was a county asylum in early Victorian times.

Clare was a happy poet. No other interpretation of the greater part of his work is possible. If we can make a distinction between poet and man, however, we must see him as a deeply unhappy man. If we can admit the psychological category known as the manic-depressive temperament, we shall have no difficulty in accepting the contradiction. The poems are the expression of his moods of exaltation; the price that was exacted for these was the fits of depression which earned him over a quarter of a century's confinement as a lunatic.

The double love of poetry and of nature has been mentioned. But it must be clear to the reader of even the fifteen poems mentioned at the beginning, and no more, that there were other currents beneath the surface of Clare's writing. To gauge these truly, it will be simplest to refer to the circumstances of his life.

The class into which John Clare was born in 1793 was a doomed one. His father, Parker Clare, was a cottage farmer. During the period of the Industrial Revolution and the Napoleonic Wars this class was obliged to struggle hopelessly against rising prices and the stranglehold of enclosure, by which means the open fields and commons where smallholders grazed their animals were legally stolen in the interest of the large landowners. The process is described with graphic indignation by Cobbett; and in the poems of Clare enclosure is the only political issue which makes any considerable intrusion. Clare's parents were permanently on the border of starvation; he himself was under-nourished, as were his own seven children, of whom only two were robust. There was always illness among them, especially consumption, through lack of food.

John was brought up in the village of Helpstone in Northamptonshire. Here he lived, apart from a move with his wife and children to Northborough, a village three miles distant, until his confinement in an asylum when he was forty-four. As a boy his pastimes were those of the other village children. Later he looked back on his childhood as a time of almost visionary happiness. It was not long before the effects of his extreme sensibility marked him out from among his companions. When he was a very small boy he was found miles from home on an expedition to find the horizon. He began to take pleasure in separating himself from his playmates, and villagers noticed that he had formed the habit of muttering to himself. Nevertheless, friendship was an important factor in his childhood, and he was deeply affected when the first friend of his boyhood died of typhus. He was still a boy when the sight of a labourer killed by falling from a haystack so shocked him that he fell into a fit which recurred periodically for years afterwards.

In boyhood too he formed a passionate attachment to a girl called Mary Joyce, four years his junior and the daughter of a well-to-do local farmer. It was she who became the ideal love who haunted his poetry and his fantasies all his life. He identified her with his Muse, the spirit of poetry and nature, the romantic vision of unattainable beauty. We know almost nothing of her except what Clare tells us. It seems that they played together as children, and that the friendship was renewed in adolescence. During adolescence and early manhood his imagination was possessed by the thought of her. It is likely that he presented himself to her as suitor, and there is no discoverable reason why they did not marry; it is not known whether she was ever in love with him, and from the worldly point of view Clare was certainly no match for an independent farmer's daughter. He never settled for long to any occupation, his parents were poor and illiterate, and he was known in the village as a queer young man of delicate constitution who scribbled verses in secret, and associated with the gipsies.

It seems that Clare gave up all hope of marrying Mary Joyce when he was about twenty-three. But he never ceased to write poems about her, passionate with regret for an unpossessed ideal. In what living form she appeared to him in the lanes near Helpstone will never be known. But in his poems she lives, now as a pastoral Muse, now as companion in childish innocence, now as a comforting presence in the horror of nightmare, finally as the spirit of unattainable perfection which racked him through his years of melancholy and mental anguish.[1]

Poetry, nature, love: these formed the triple constellation by which the tempestuous course of Clare's life was directed. What he was looking for, throughout his communion with nature and with the tortured fantasies of his own mind, was above all, love. The note of poignancy, the pure and tender wistfulness which haunts all his nature poetry arises from self-pity; self-pity is the expression of a desire for love. When Clare writes from his sympathy with small and helpless creatures, he is really thinking of himself. He projects his own nature on to the defenceless snail, the bee searching wearily for honey, the happy lark, the timid water bird, and, when he was feeling beaten and persecuted, the hunted badger.[2] Such identifications are, of course, unconscious. If Clare's self-pity had been evident to himself, it would not arouse our sympathy. His whole life was a dogged struggle against the causes of his discontent; in the end it cost him his liberty, if not his sanity.

When he was still a schoolboy, Clare fell in love with poetry. It was for years a secret delight, of which he seemed ashamed. He saved his pennies and bought books of poetry in the

[1] Of one of his dream experiences Clare wrote: 'These dreams of a beautiful presence, a woman deity, gave the sublimest conceptions of beauty to my imagination; and being last night with the same presence, the lady divinity left such a vivid picture of her visits in my sleep, dreaming of dreams, that I could no longer doubt her existence. So I wrote them down to prolong the happiness of my faith in believing her my guardian genius.'

[2] See the poem on the badger (p. 92). For this suggestion I am indebted to *John Clare: a Life* (Cobden Sanderson, 1932) by J. W. and Anne Tibble. From this and from the same editors, *The Letters of John Clare* (Routlege and Kegan Paul, 1951) I have obtained all the biographical material in this introduction.

nearest market towns. He began to make up rhymes himself and write them down in secret on any scraps of paper he could find, sugar bags for instance. These were stored in a hole in the chimney of his parents' cottage. Some were unwittingly destroyed by his mother. He was ashamed of poetry because it was not the sort of interest thought proper for a village labourer's child. When his secret became known in the family, his mother was sympathetic in encouraging the boy's oddity. In the sketches which he left for his unfinished autobiography Clare says: 'I cannot say what led me to dabble in rhyme.' In this artless sentence there is a touch of tragic irony. There never was a more helpless and more completely possessed victim of poetry. If he had known why he was destined to be a poet, if he had been conscious of the reason for his bondage, he might have been less a victim. He knew only that when the 'rhyming' fit was on, there was no resisting it. He wrote because he could not help it; poetry was his only constant occupation. He tried his hand at many country trades, but he never stayed for long at any of them. The writing of verse came to him easily and naturally, yet he never found the writing of prose easy. He had to master consciously the art of prose syntax. It was as if, without rhyme and metre, he was a ship without chart or rudder. He never learnt to spell uniformly, and he could not punctuate at all.

The desire for fame was never so naïve and rapturous with Clare as it was with his contemporary, Keats. It took the form rather of a sober desire for recognition, the natural wish that his prowess as a poet should be judged by those considered competent to judge, and measured against those whose reputations were established. By the time he was twenty-four he had written a considerable amount of verse, and he began to think of ways of getting it published. At that time the normal way to bring this about was to issue a printed prospectus, display it in bookshops or hawk it from door to door, and collect subscriptions sufficient to justify the cost of printing. Clare hardly knew how to set about this, but at length his prospectus was issued. It was a failure. A year or two later, however, it was noticed by a local bookseller, who immediately showed an interest in Clare's poems; he was cousin to John Taylor, a London bookseller (the term 'publisher' was not used until later). At length, in 1820, when Clare was nearly twenty-seven, his first book of poems was published in London. It was an immediate and enormous success. Four editions were called for in the year. The literary world was united in its praise of the peasant-poet from Northamptonshire.

Looking back over the whole story, a modern reader cannot help regarding this triumph as a disaster for Clare. He was for a time the object of widespread interest from *littérateurs*, county squires, fashionable visitors from London and local parsons. Their interest was philanthropic rather than strictly poetical. This was because Taylor had done his work too well. He had assured the success of the poems in advance by harping loudly on the strain of the 'peasant-poet,' to Clare's own considerable annoyance. What Clare received was less critical attention to his poetry than charitable concern for his poverty. It was an age of charity, and everybody meant well. As the result of appeals by genuinely philanthropic patrons a fund was raised which was sufficient to keep the peasant-poet—and the family he began to raise—just below the subsistence level. Unfortunately the interest which Taylor had stirred up so effectively was almost as quick to subside. A second volume of poems issued the following year sold badly. His third and fourth volumes appeared in 1827 and 1835 and failed.

The story of the years that followed Clare's triumph is one of dogged persistence in trying to earn a livelihood, refusal to accept the loss of recognition, acute economic worry, and throughout everything, increased mastery of the poet's art. The destruction of the man followed remorselessly, as the triumph of the poet proceeded. In 1817, after his hopes of marrying Mary were defeated, Clare had met and begun to court Martha Turner, the daughter of a small farmer. This was Patty, whom he married in 1820 when her pregnancy could no longer be hidden. With her he lived in utter poverty amidst an increasing family of ailing children, until his removal to an asylum after seventeen years. What we know of Patty we have only from Clare himself. She could have had no strength and time to be more than a provider for her family.

She knew no more of poetry than the average farmers daughter, and she could do nothing to satisfy the poet's craving for ideal companionship and understanding. Clare's needs were not to be met from ordinary human resources. In his letters he speaks of her with alternate displeasure and tenderness, according to his moods. He was an impossible husband for a woman in her position. The economic circumstances of the family are the key to the story at this point. Clare's sudden rise to literary fame effectively cut him off from the community of the village from which his genius had already tended to separate him.[1] Farmers would not employ as day-labourer a man who might be called from the fields at any moment to wash his hands in response to a visit from some titled bigwig in his private coach. Yet the receipts from his literary work were never enough to combat rising prices and the needs of a growing family. There was a general slump in the sales of poetry. Many of the magazines which were glad enough to print Clare's poems forgot to pay for them. Taylor, whatever his will and intentions, managed Clare's money disastrously. His was a somewhat complicated nature, which it would be wrong to judge harshly. He probably did not cheat Clare of his earnings deliberately, but the record of his book-keeping is not creditable to him. What it is difficult to forgive Taylor and the others of Clare's patrons in the world of literature and fashion is their failure to understand his economic need; this was for no more than a competent handling of his affairs to enable him to gain a small though regular income. The part that simple financial anxiety can play in mental collapse was less generally understood then that it is now. It was, however, the opinion expressed by Dr. Allen, keeper of the private asylum where Clare was first confined, that all that was needed to restore his mental balance was the assurance of a regular income, however small. To this Clare's published writings entitled

[1] 'I live here among the ignorant like a lost man in fact like one whom the rest seems careless of having anything to do with—they hardly dare talk in my company for fear I should mention them in my writings & I find more pleasure in wandering the fields then in mixing among my silent neighbours who are insensible of everything but toiling & talking of it & that to no purpose.' (Fom a letter to Taylor, February 8, 1822.)

him, had his affairs been efficiently managed. But Dr. Allen was a psychiatrist before his time.

Clare's health was never good. Over-excitement and excessive mental activity were succeeded by fits of melancholia and nervous depression. The relief he sought did him no permanent good, and probably little harm. He began to suffer from delusions. His egotism, inflamed by lack of due recognition, expressed itself in a tendency to identify himself with other great poets, especially Byron, whose romantic death in 1824 was felt throughout the country, not only in literary circles. Undoubtedly Clare suffered from a suppressed sense of social inferiority; however much he professed his sturdy independence, he was never a radical, yet the presence of rank always made him acutely embarrassed. When fashionable coaches rolled up to his cottage door, he preferred to disappear through the back garden if he could do so safely. He was patronised in the most condescending manner by his titled landlord. The patronage was well-meant, and Clare never expressly resented it. But there are outbursts of irritation at the enforced status of peasant poet. How tempting, then, and how natural, in periods of mental derangement, to identify himself with Lord Byron—rich, titled, famous, a great lover and a hero. Famous prize-fighters were other objects of his self-projection. He was small and his father had been a man of such physical strength that he was chosen for the strenuous work of threshing. As a volunteer in the militia that was assembled to meet the threatened invasion of Napoleon, Clare had been so riled by the jeers of his sergeant that he had knocked him down. He was pugnacious by nature, but not quarrelsome. Of interest, in the circumstances, is his attempt to publish in literary magazines imitations of the writings of dead poets, such as Sir Henry Wotton, and pass them off as genuine. Minor literary forgery was not uncommon at this time; it was a harmless attempt to exercise his literary powers, from which candid friends succeeded in dissuading him. Yet it was a dangerous manifestation in one already beginning to have delusions about his identity.

When a man has been certified insane, it is not difficult to discover in his actions the evidence for insanity. Most people generally considered sane are capable of isolated actions or words, particularly at moments of stress, which could be interpreted as those of an insane person. If a person is under an emotional or nervous strain which becomes excessive, he takes refuge in disordered words or conduct which express his feelings and relieve the strain. Insanity becomes a refuge. Clare's instability was of this nature. He held out against it for eight more years after all reasonable hope of making a living as a writer had failed. His actions grew more and more strange; his pain and suffering increased; his mental aberrations, his delusions, his fits of melancholy and depression became more frequent and more incalculable. In 1837, alarmed for his health, his friends had him removed to High Beech private asylum in Epping Forest.

Here he remained for four years. He was found to be quiet and harmless; he was wisely discouraged from writing much poetry [1] An improvement in his material circumstances would probably have cured him. But while the physical and spiritual causes of his malady remained, no cure was possible. In a sense his circumstances were aggravated by removal, because he continued to worry about his family who were now many miles away. He wanted security, home and companionship. For these he might have pined indefinitely. But in the summer of 1841 he ran away.

The story of his four days' tramp home, as described afterwards by himself, is one of the most pitiful ever told. It represents perhaps the culmination of his tragedy. It was his last hopeless attempt for freedom. He was continually on the point of collapse from exhaustion. His shoes wore out, but he dragged himself along on tortured feet. He had nothing

[1] The longest poem of this period, *Child Harold*, is printed in full for the first time in Mr. Geoffrey Grigson's *Poems of John Clare's Madness*, and contains many moving passages, of which the following is one:

Life is to me a dream that never wakes:
Night finds me on this lengthening road alone.
Love is to me a thought that ever aches,
A frost-bound thought that freezes life to stone.
Mary, in truth and nature still my own,
That warms the winter of my aching breast,
Thy name is joy, nor will I life bemoan.
Midnight, when sleep takes charge of nature's rest,
Finds me awake and friendless—not distrest.

to eat or drink except the grass by the roadside and what he could buy with the penny thrown to him by a passing labourer. At length, as he neared his own village, a woman with some children in a cart forced him to get in beside them. It was his wife Patty, and he did not recognise her. In describing the incident, he refers to her as 'my second wife Patty.' It was one of his constant delusions at this time and during the succeeding years that Patty was his second, and Mary his first, wife. Just before his escape from High Beech he wrote a letter which begins:

MY DEAR WIFE MARY,—I might have said my first wife first love & first everything—but I shall never forget my second wife & second love for I loved her once as dearly as yourself & almost do so now so I determined to keep you both for ever—and when I write to you I am writing to her at the same time & in the same letter God bless you both for ever & both your families also. . . .

The woman to whom this letter was written had died unmarried three years before.

Clare remained at home for only six months. He relapsed into his former condition. The local gentry were disturbed that a man of such irrational and incalculable temperament should be at large in their midst. At their instance he was certified insane, and removed for the rest of his life to Northampton General Lunatic Asylum. From now until his death in 1864 he lived more and more in a purely mental world, though at least until 1850 he seems to have had hopes of returning home. At first he was allowed considerable liberty and was treated in the town as a harmless lunatic. Visitors came to see and talk to him. They often went away with copies of new poems. Most of them found evidences in his conversation of the insanity they came to look for. The old delusions persisted. He was Lord Byron; some of his best lines had been stolen by poets now dead. After some years he was shut up in the Asylum grounds and kept away from the town; this was not because of any change in his behaviour but because of a new régime. He continued to write poems, among them some of his best and most moving. The last thirty-seven poems in this selection were written during the period following his removal to High Beech in 1837. At

Northampton he corresponded very little with the outside world. The last letter we possess was addressed to an unknown inquirer and is dated 1860. It is as follows:

DEAR SIR,—I am in a Madhouse & quite forget your Name or who you are. You must excuse me for I have nothing to communicate or tell of & why I am shut up I dont know I have nothing to say so I conclude

Yours respectfully

JOHN CLARE

V

FOR the last twenty-seven years of his life Clare was treated as a lunatic. By the standards of his day he was a madman. We may accept this if we are prepared to regard madness, not as a clearly defined state, in all cases alike, but as a condition of mind which requires, for the sake of its possessor, of his family and associates, or of society in general, special treatment. Clare was ill. If he could have commanded the skilled devotion of a loving and loved companion, there would have been no need for Northampton Asylum. What appals us in the story of Clare's agony is its length, the comparative ease with which it could be relieved nowadays, and the utter helplessness of its victim. He did not know what was happening to him; no one with any power to act knew.

Clare was ill, but not incurably or permanently. The utterances of his sanity far outweigh those of his madness. Poetically he was not mad; many of the utterances which visitors found evidence of madness were poetically sane, the fictions of that imagination of which 'the lunatic, the lover and the poet are all compact.' The letter to Mary Joyce quoted above is not insane; it is poetically true and just—Clare loved equally the real and the ideal woman. Nor is his remark to the visitor about Gray insane: 'I know Gray,' he said, 'I know him well.' Any poet, any reader with imaginative insight, *knows* the writers he loves; time means nothing to him. He knows a fellow poet, of whatever epoch, better than he knows his neighbour, if the poet is a kindred spirit and the neighbour a dull boor.

The story of Clare's life must be read along with the poems. If we feel that society, or destiny, dealt unmercifully with him, we can make some amend by reading his poems with care and understanding. Madness, frustration, and spiritual shipwreck were the offerings Clare made to destiny in exchange for his poems. These, with all their faults, are the justification for his sufferings. Were the sufferings necessary for the creation of the poems? Would relief from suffering have destroyed them? In the deepest sense, the answer to these questions must be Yes. For the poems were the outcome and the expression of happiness; even when they express misery, despair and frustration, as they often do with the utmost poignancy, their composition is Clare's triumph over suffering. The writing of a fully expressive poem, whatever the theme, can only bring the true poet happiness. Happiness and suffering have their origin in the same cause—an excess of feeling, sudden or gradual, brief or long-lasting. The dividing line is soon crossed. The poet's abnormal sensibility makes him a pioneer in feeling, painful or pleasant; the value of poetry lies in its discovery of new emotion. A potential poet who finds that excess of sensibility is too much for him turns away from poetry. The ordinary person, finding emotion excessive, takes refuge in conventional habits of feeling and in common contentment. Contentment blunts sensibility, or at any rate puts it safely to sleep. Clare might have taken refuge from excessive sensibility in irresponsible madness. He took refuge in occasional madness as he had early taken refuge in riotous company. Neither of these expedients served, because he was a poet, and so committed to the exercise of sensibility, however painful, however intolerable. His life was courageous throughout. His courage was not exactly moral courage, it was a courage half spiritual and half animal, like that of a hunted creature or a bird defending its nest. 'I am in a mad-house and . . . why I am shut up I don't know.' The very calmness with which these words are written, with all their terrible implications, is in itself spiritual fortitude in the extreme.

Henry Crabbe Robinson, recording a meeting with him on a visit to London in 1824, commented: 'Clare looks like a weak man, but he was ill.' Clare was in many ways a weak man ; and the greater his weakness, the greater his courage. For by the end of his long life he had finally put aside all the temptations to which his overstrained spirit had often yielded, temptations to deny his manhood and lose his identity in dreams, nightmares, delusions, hallucinations, impersonations. When he wrote his triumphant affirmation *I Am*, he was reconciled to the burden of identity which in religious language is called the soul and by which alone man is man. Some are ready to lose most of their identity in one of the world's convenient disguises; Clare regained his and possessed it at the end, even though in doing so he possessed nothing besides.

As a record of human tragedy Clare's life is one of the most poignant stories we possess in detail. Yet in reading it we should be careful in apportioning blame for the tragedy, which is one of misplaced well-wishing and well-intentioned ignorance rather than of deliberate injury or malice. Given Clare's nature and its social context, the tragedy was probable, if not inevitable. The destruction of the man was the triumph of the poet. Whether the destruction was necessary is a matter for speculation. There is no reader who would not, on the score of compassion, sacrifice some at least of the poetry if it could have mitigated the tragedy. But out of Clare's unhappiness, as well as his happiness, sprang the poems. If we esteem the poems, we must accept the unhappiness. Things had to be as they were—if not in detail, at least in their general plan. The general plan of Clare's life was something which we cannot help feeling was fixed by forces outside the control of either the victim or of the well-meaning mortal agents who surrounded him.

J. R.

Chalfont St. Giles
1953

POEMS

NOON

ALL how silent and how still,
Nothing heard but yonder mill;
While the dazzled eye surveys
All around a liquid blaze;
And amid the scorching gleams,
If we earnest look, it seems
As if crooked bits of glass
Seem'd repeatedly to pass.
Oh, for a puffing breeze to blow!
But breezes are all strangers now;
Not a twig is seen to shake
Nor the smallest bent to quake;
From the river's muddy side
Not a curve is seen to glide;
And no longer on the stream
Watching lies the silver bream,
Forcing, from repeated springs,
'Verges in successive rings.'
Bees are faint, and cease to hum;
Birds are overpower'd and dumb.
Rural voices all are mute,
Tuneless lie the pipe and flute;
Shepherds, with their panting sheep,
In the swaliest corner creep;
And from the tormenting heat
All are wishing to retreat.
Huddled up in grass and flowers,
Mowers wait for cooler hours;
And the cow-boy seeks the sedge,
Ramping in the woodland hedge,
While his cattle o'er the vales
Scamper, with uplifted tails;
Others not so wild and mad,
That can better bear the gad,
Underneath the hedgerow lunge,
Or, if nigh, in waters plunge.
Oh! to see how flowers are took,
How it grieves me when I look:

1

Ragged-robins, once so pink,
Now are turn'd as black as ink,
And the leaves, being scorch'd so much,
Even crumble at the touch;
Drowking lies the meadow-sweet,
Flopping down beneath one's feet;
While to all the flowers that blow,
If in open air they grow,
Th'injurious deed alike is done
By the hot relentless sun.
E'en the dew is parched up
From the teasel's jointed cup:
O poor birds! where must ye fly,
Now your water-pots are dry?
If ye stay upon the heath,
Ye'll be chok'd and clamm'd to death:
Therefore leave the shadeless goss,
Seek the spring-head lin'd with moss;
There your little feet may stand,
Safely printing on the sand;
While, in full possession, where
Purling eddies ripple clear,
You with ease and plenty blest,
Sip the coolest and the best.
Then away! and wet your throats;
Cheer me with your warbling notes;
'Twill hot noon the more revive;
While I wander to contrive
For myself a place as good,
In the middle of a wood:
There aside some mossy bank,
Where the grass in bunches rank
Lifts its down on spindles high,
Shall be where I'll choose to lie;
Fearless of the things that creep,
There I'll think, and there I'll sleep,
Caring not to stir at all,
Till the dew begins to fall.

1809.

IMPROMPTU ON WINTER

O WINTER, what a deadly foe
Art thou unto the mean and low!
What thousands now half-pin'd and bare
Are forced to stand thy piercing air
All day, near numbed to death wi' cold
Some petty gentry to uphold,
Paltry proudlings hard as thee,
Dead to all humanity.
Oh, the weather's cold and snow,
Cutting winds that round me blow,
But much more the killing scorn!
Oh, the day that I was born
Friendless—poor as I can be,
Struck wi' death o' poverty!
But why need I the winter blame?
To me all seasons come the same:
Now winter bares each field and tree
She finds that trouble sav'd in me
Stript already, penniless,
Nothing boasting but distress;
And when spring chill'd nature cheers,
Still my old complaint she hears;
Summer too, in plenty blest,
Finds me poor and still distrest;
Kind autumn too, so liberal and so free,
Brings my old well-known present, Poverty.
                                   1809–10.

THE WOOD-CUTTER'S NIGHT SONG

WELCOME, red and roundy sun,
    Dropping lowly in the west;
Now my hard day's work is done,
    I'm as happy as the best.

Joyful are the thoughts of home,
    Now I'm ready for my chair,
So, till morrow-morning's come,
    Bill and mittens, lie ye there!

3

Though to leave your pretty song,
   Little birds, it gives me pain,
Yet to-morrow is not long,
   Then I'm with you all again.

If I stop, and stand about,
   Well I know how things will be,
Judy will be looking out
   Every now-and-then for me.

So fare-ye-well! and hold your tongues,
   Sing no more until I come;
They're not worthy of your songs
   That never care to drop a crumb.

All day long I love the oaks,
   But, at nights, yon little cot,
Where I see the chimney smokes,
   Is by far the prettiest spot.

Wife and children all are there,
   To revive with pleasant looks,
Table ready set, and chair,
   Supper hanging on the hooks.

Soon as ever I get in,
   When my faggot down I fling,
Little prattlers they begin
   Teasing me to talk and sing.

Welcome, red and roundy sun,
   Dropping lowly in the west;
Now my hard day's work is done,
   I'm as happy as the best.

Joyful are the thoughts of home,
   Now I'm ready for my chair,
So, till morrow-morning's come,
   Bill and mittens, lie ye there!

4

RECOLLECTIONS AFTER AN EVENING WALK

JUST as the even-bell rang, we set out
To wander the fields and the meadows about;
And the first thing we mark'd that was lovely to view
Was the sun hung on nothing, just bidding adieu:
He seem'd like a ball of pure gold in the west,
In a cloud like a mountain blue, dropping to rest;
The skies all around him were ting'd with his rays,
And the trees at a distance seem'd all on a blaze,
Till, lower and lower, he sank from our sight,
And the blue mist came creeping with silence and night.
The woodman then ceas'd with his hatchet to hack,
And bent away home with his kid on his back;
The mower, too, lapt up his scythe from our sight,
And put on his jacket, and bid us good night;
The thresher once lumping, we heard him no more,
He left his barn-dust, and had shut up his door;
The shepherd had told all his sheep in his pen,
And humming his song, sought his cottage agen:
But the sweetest of all seeming music to me
Were the songs of the clumsy brown-beetle and bee;
The one was seen hast'ning away to his hive,
The other was just from his sleeping alive—
'Gainst our hats he kept knocking as if he'd no eyes,
And when batter'd down he was puzzled to rise.
The little gay moth, too, was lovely to view,
A-dancing with lily-white wings in the dew;
He whisk'd o'er the water-pudge flirting and airy,
And perch'd on the down-headed grass like a fairy.
And there came the snail from his shell peeping out,
As fearful and cautious as thieves on the rout;
The sly jumping frog, too, had ventur'd to tramp,
And the glow-worm had just 'gun to light up his lamp;
To sip of the dew the worm peep'd from his den,
But dreading our footsteps soon vanish'd agen:
And numbers of creatures appear'd in our sight,
That live in the silence and sweetness of night,
Climbing up the tall grasses or scaling the bough,
But these were all nameless, unnotic'd till now.

And then we wound round 'neath the brook's willow row,
And look'd at the clouds that kept passing below;
The moon's image too, in the brook we could see't,
As if 'twas the other world under our feet;
And we listen'd well pleas'd at the guggles and groans
The water made passing the pebbles and stones.
And then we turn'd up by the rut-rifted lane,
And sought for our cot and the village again;
For night gather'd round, and shut all from the eye,
And a black sultry cloud crept all over the sky;
The dew on the bush, soon as touch'd it would drop,
And the grass 'neath our feet was as wet as a mop:
And, as to the town we approach'd very fast,
The bat even popp'd in our face as he past;
And the crickets sang loud as we went by the house,
And by the barn-side we saw many a mouse
Quirking round for the kernels that, litter'd about,
Were shook from the straw which the thresher hurl'd
    out.
And then we came up to our cottage once more,
And shut out the night-dew, and lock'd up the door;
The dog bark'd a welcome, well-pleas'd at our sight,
And the owl o'er our cot flew, and whoop'd a 'good
    night.'

AN EFFUSION TO POESY

ON RECEIVING A DAMP FROM A GENTEEL OPINIONIST
IN POETRY, OF SOME SWAY, AS I AM TOLD, IN THE
LITERARY WORLD

Despis'd, unskill'd, or how I will,
Sweet Poesy! I'll love thee still;
Vain (cheering comfort!) though I be,
I still must love thee, Poesy.
A poor, rude clown, and what of that?
I cannot help the will of fate,
A lowly clown although I be;
Nor can I help it loving thee.

6

Still must I love thee, sweetest charm!
Still must my soul in raptures warm;
Still must my rudeness pluck the flower,
That's plucked in an evil hour,
While Learning scowls her scornful brow,
And damps my soul—I know not how.
Labour! 'cause thou'rt mean and poor,
Learning spurns thee from her door;
But despise me as she will,
Poesy! I love thee still.
When on pillow'd thorns I weep,
And vainly stretch me down to sleep,
Then, thou charm from heav'n above,
Comfort's cordial dost thou prove:
Then, engaging Poesy!
Then how sweet to talk with thee.
And be despis'd, or how I will,
I cannot help but love thee still.
Endearing charm! vain though I be,
I still must love thee, Poesy.
Still must I! ay, I can't refrain:
Damp'd, despis'd, or scorn'd again,
With vain, unhallow'd liberty
Still must I sing thee, Poesy.
And poor, and vain, and press'd beneath
Oppression's scorn although I be,
Still will I bind my simple wreath,
Still will I love thee, Poesy.

RECOLLECTIONS AFTER A RAMBLE

THE rosy day was sweet and young,
    The clod-brown lark that hail'd the morn
Had just his summer anthem sung,
    And trembling dropped in the corn;
The dew-rais'd flower was perk and proud,
    The butterfly around it play'd;
The skies blew clear, save woolly cloud
    That pass'd the sun without a shade.

7

On the pismire's castle hill,
　　While the burnet-buttons quak'd,
While beside the stone-pav'd rill
　　Cowslip bunches nodding shak'd,
Bees in every peep did try,
　　Great had been the honey shower,
Soon their load was on their thigh,
　　Yellow dust as fine as flour.

Brazen magpies, fond of clack,
　　Full of insolence and pride,
Chattering on the donkey's back
　　Percht, and pull'd his shaggy hide;
Odd crows settled on the pad,
　　Dames from milking trotting home
Said no sign was half so sad,
　　And shook their heads at ills to come.

While cows restless from the ground
　　Plung'd into the stream and drank,
And the rings went whirling round,
　　Till they toucht the flaggy bank,
On the arch's wall I knelt,
　　Curious, as I often did,
To see the words the sculpture spelt,
　　But the moss its letters hid.

Labour sought the water cool,
　　And stretching took a hearty sup,
The fish were playing in the pool,
　　And turn'd their milk-white bellies up;
Clothes laid down behind a bush,
　　Boys were wading near the pad,
Deeply did the maiden blush
　　As she pass'd each naked lad.

Some with lines the fish to catch,
　　Quirking boys let loose from school
Others 'side the hedgerow watch,
　　Where the linnet took the wool:

8

'Tending Hodge had slept too fast,
  While his cattle stray'd abroad,
Swift the freed horse gallop'd past,
  Pattering down the stony road.

The gipsies' tune was loud and strong,
  As round the camp they danc'd a jig,
And much I lov'd the brown girl's song,
  While list'ning on the wooden brig;
The shepherd, he was on his rounds,
  The dog stopt short to lap the stream,
And jingling in the fallow grounds
  The ploughman urg'd his reeking team.

Often did I stop to gaze
  On each spot once dear to me,
Known 'mong those remember'd days
  Of banish'd, happy infancy:
Often did I view the shade
  Where once a nest my eyes did fill,
And often mark'd the place I play'd
  At 'roly-poly' down the hill.

In the wood's deep shade did stand,
  As I pass'd, the sticking-troop;
And Goody begg'd a helping hand
  To heave her rotten faggot up:
The riding-gate, sharp jerking round,
  Follow'd fast my heels again,
While echo mockt the clapping sound,
  And 'clap, clap,' sang the woods amain.

The wood is sweet—I love it well,
  In spending there my leisure hours,
To seek the snail its painted shell,
  And look about for curious flowers;
Or 'neath the hazel's leafy thatch,
  On a stulp or mossy ground,
Little squirrel's gambols watch,
  Dancing oak trees round and round.

9

Green was the shade—I love the woods,
When autumn's wind is mourning loud,
To see the leaves float on the floods,
Dead within their yellow shroud:
The wood was then in glory spread—
I love the browning bough to see
That litters autumn's dying bed—
Her latest sigh is dear to me.

'Neath a spreading shady oak
For a while to muse I lay;
From its grains a bough I broke,
To fan the teasing flies away:
Then I sought the woodland side,
Cool the breeze my face did meet,
And the shade the sun did hide;
Though 'twas hot, it seemed sweet.

And as while I clomb the hill,
Many a distant charm I found,
Pausing on the lagging mill,
That scarcely mov'd its sails around,
Hanging o'er a gate or stile,
Till my curious eye did tire,
Leisure was employ'd awhile,
Counting many a peeping spire.

While the hot sun 'gan to wane,
Cooling glooms fast deep'ning still,
Refreshing greenness spread the plain,
As black clouds crept the southern hill;
Labour sought a sheltering place,
'Neath some thick wood-woven bower,
While odd rain-drops dampt his face,
Heralds of the coming shower.

Where the oak-plank cross'd the stream,
Which the early-rising lass
Climbs with milk-pail gathering cream,
Crook'd paths tracking through the grass:

10

There, where willows hing their boughs,
    Briers and blackthorns form'd a bower
Stunted thick by sheep and cows—
    There I stood to shun the shower.

Sweet it was to feel the breeze
    Blowing cool without the sun,
Bumming gad-flies ceas'd to tease,
    All seem'd glad the shower to shun:
Sweet it was to mark the flower,
    Rain-drops glist'ning on its head,
Perking up beneath the bower,
    As if rising from the dead.

And full sweet it was to look,
    How clouds misted o'er the hill,
Rain-drops how they dimpt the brook,
    Falling fast and faster still;
While the gudgeons sturting by
    Cring'd 'neath water-grasses' shade,
Startling as each nimble eye
    Saw the rings the dropples made.

And upon the dripping ground,
    As the shower had ceas'd again,
As the eye was wandering round,
    Trifling troubles caus'd a pain;
Overtaken in the shower,
    Bumble-bees I wander'd by,
Clinging to the drowking flower,
    Left without the power to fly:

And full often, drowning wet,
    Scampering beetles rac'd away,
Safer shelter glad to get,
    Drownded out from whence they lay:
While the moth, for night's reprief,
    Waited safe and snug withal
'Neath the plantain's bowery leaf,
    Where not e'en a drop could fall.

11

Then the clouds dispers'd again,
　And full sweet it was to view
Sunbeams, trembling long in vain,
　Now they 'gan to glimmer through:
And as labour strength regains
　From ale's booning bounty given,
So reviv'd the fresh'ning plains
　From the smiling showers of heaven.

Sweet the birds did chant their songs,
　Blackbird, linnet, lark, and thrush;
Music from a many tongues
　Melted from each dripping bush:
Deafen'd echo, on the plain,
　As the sunbeams broke the cloud,
Scarce could help repeat the strain,
　Nature's anthem flow'd so loud.

What a fresh'ning feeling came,
　As the sun's smile gleam'd again;
Sultry summer wa'n't the same,
　Such a mildness swept the plain;
Breezes, such as one would seek,
　Cooling infants of the shower,
Fanning sweet the burning cheek,
　Trembled through the bramble-bower.

Insects of mysterious birth
　Sudden struck my wondering sight,
Doubtless brought by moisture forth,
　Hid in knots of spittle white;
Backs of leaves the burthen bear,
　Where the sunbeams cannot stray,
'Wood-seers' call'd, that wet declare,
　So the knowing shepherds say.

As the cart-rut rippled down
　With the burden of the rain,
Boys came drabbling from the town,
　Glad to meet their sports again;

Stopping up the mimic rills,
　　Till they forc'd their frothy bound,
Then the keck-made water-mills
　　In the current whisk'd around.

Once again did memory pain
　　O'er the life she once had led;
Once did manhood wish again
　　Childish joys had never fled:
'Could I lay these woes aside
　　Which I long have murmur'd o'er,
Mix a boy with boys,' I sigh'd,
　　'Fate should then be teas'd no more.'

Hot the sun in summer warms,
　　Quick the roads dry o'er the plain:
Girls, with baskets on their arms,
　　Soon renew'd their sports again;
O'er the green they sought their play,
　　Where the cowslip-bunches grew,
Quick the rush-bent fann'd away,
　　As they danc'd and bounded through.

Some went searching by the wood,
　　Peeping 'neath the weaving thorn,
Where the pouch-lipp'd cuckoo-bud
　　From its snug retreat was torn;
Where the ragged-robin grew
　　With its pip'd stem streak'd with jet,
And the crow-flower's golden hue
　　Careless plenty easier met.

Some, with many an anxious pain
　　Childish wishes to pursue,
From the pond-head gaz'd in vain
　　On the flag-flower's yellow hue,
Smiling in its safety there,
　　Sleeping o'er its shadow'd blow,
While the flood's triumphing care
　　Crimpled round its root below.

Then I stood to pause again;
    Retrospection sigh'd and smil'd,
Musing, 'tween a joy and pain,
    How I acted when a child;
When by clearing brooks I've been,
    Where the painted sky was given,
Thinking, if I tumbled in,
    I should fall direct to heaven.

Many an hour had come and gone
    Since the town last met my eye,
Where, huge baskets mauling on,
    Maids hung out their clothes to dry;
Granny there was on the bench,
    Coolly sitting in the swale,
Stopping oft a love-sick wench,
    To pinch her snuff, and hear her tale.

Be the journey e'er so mean,
    Passing by a cot or tree,
In the route there's something seen
    Which the curious love to see;
In each ramble, taste's warm souls
    More of wisdom's self can view
Than blind ignorance beholds
    All life's seven stages through.

TO AN INFANT DAUGHTER

SWEET gem of infant fairy-flowers!
Thy smiles on life's unclosing hours,
Like sunbeams lost in summer showers,
        They wake my fears;
When reason knows its sweets and sours,
        They'll change to tears.

God help thee, little senseless thing!
Thou, daisy-like of early spring,

Of ambush'd winter's hornet sting
    Hast yet to tell;
Thou know'st not what to-morrows bring:
    I wish thee well.

But thou art come, and soon or late
'Tis thine to meet the frowns of fate,
The harpy grin of envy's hate,
    And mermaid-smiles
Of worldly folly's luring bait,
    That youth beguiles.

And much I wish, whate'er may be
The lot, my child, that falls to thee,
Nature may never let thee see
    Her glass betimes,
But keep thee from my failings free—
    Nor itch at rhymes.

Lord help thee in thy coming years
If thy mad father's picture 'pears
Predominant!—his feeling fears
    And jingling starts;
I'd freely now gi' vent to tears
    To ease my heart.

May thou, unknown to rhyming bother,
Be ignorant as is thy mother,
And in thy manners such another,
    Save sin's nigh quest;
And then with 'scaping this and t'other
    Thou mayst be blest.[1]

Lord knows my heart, it loves thee much;
And may my feelings, aches, and such,
The pains I meet in folly's clutch
    Be never thine:
Child, it's a tender string to touch,
    That sounds 'Thou'rt mine.'

[1] Preceding two verses added from MS.

15

TO POESY

O SWEETLY wild and witching Poesy !
  Thou light of this world's hermitage I prove thee;
And surely none helps loving thee that knows thee,
  A soul of feeling cannot help but love thee.
I would say how thy secret wonders move me,
  Thou spell of loveliness!—but 'tis too much:
Had I the language of the gods above me
  I might then venture thy wild harp to touch,
And sing of all thy thrilling pains and pleasures,
  The flowers I meet in this world's wilderness,
The comforts rising from thy spell-bound treasures,
  Thy cordial balm that softens my distress:
I would say all, but thou art far above me;
  Words are too weak, expression can't be had;
I can but say I love, and dearly love thee,
  And that thou cheer'st me when my soul is sad.

TO THE IVY

DARK creeping Ivy, with thy berries brown,
  That fondly twists on ruins all thine own,
Old spire-points studding with a leafy crown
  Which every minute threatens to dethrone;
With fearful eye I view thy height sublime,
  And oft with quicker step retreat from thence
Where thou, in weak defiance, striv'st with Time,
  And hold'st his weapons in a dread suspense.
But, bloom of ruins, thou art dear to me,
  When, far from danger's way, thy gloomy pride
Wreathes picturesque around some ancient tree
  That bows his branches by some fountain-side:
Then sweet it is from summer suns to be,
With thy green darkness overshadowing me.

NATURE

O SIMPLE Nature, how I do delight
  To pause upon thy trifles—foolish things,
As some would call them. On the summer night,
  Tracing the lane-path where the dog-rose hings
  With dew-drops seeth'd, while chick'ring cricket sings,
My eye can't help but glance upon its leaves,
  Where love's warm beauty steals her sweetest blush,
When, soft the while, the even silent heaves
  Her pausing breath just trembling thro' the bush,
  And then again dies calm, and all is hush.
Oh, how I feel, just as I pluck the flower
  And stick it to my breast—words can't reveal;
But there are souls that in this lovely hour
  Know all I mean, and feel whate'er I feel.

SUMMER

How sweet, when weary, dropping on a bank,
  Turning a look around on things that be!
E'en feather-headed grasses, spindling rank,
  A-trembling to the breeze one loves to see;
  And yellow buttercup, where many a bee
Comes buzzing to its head and bows it down;
  And the great dragon-fly with gauzy wings,
In gilded coat of purple, green, or brown,
  That on broad leaves of hazel basking clings,
  Fond of the sunny day—and other things
Past counting, please me while thus here I lie.
  But still reflective pains are not forgot:
Summer sometime shall bless this spot, when I,
  Hapt in the cold dark grave, can heed it not.

A COPSE IN WINTER

SHADES, though you're leafless, save the bramble-spear,
  Whose weather-beaten leaves, of purple stain,
In hardy stubbornness cling all the year
  To their old thorns, till spring buds new again;

Shades, still I love you better than the plain,
    For here I find the earliest flowers that blow,
While on the bare blea bank do yet remain
    Old winter's traces, little heaps of snow.
    Beneath your ashen roots, primroses grow
From dead grass tufts and matted moss, once more;
    Sweet beds of violets dare again be seen
In their deep purple pride; and, gay display'd,
    The crow-flowers, creeping from the naked green,
Add early beauties to your sheltering shade.

NOON

The midday hour of twelve the clock counts o'er,
    A sultry stillness lulls the air asleep;
The very buzz of flies is heard no more,
    Nor faintest wrinkles o'er the waters creep.
Like one large sheet of glass the pool does shine,
    Reflecting in its face the burnt sunbeam:
The very fish their sturting play decline,
    Seeking the willow-shadows 'side the stream.
And, where the hawthorn branches o'er the pool,
    The little bird, forsaking song and nest,
Flutters on dripping twigs his limbs to cool,
    And splashes in the stream his burning breast.
Oh, free from thunder, for a sudden shower,
To cherish nature in this noonday hour!

WRITTEN IN NOVEMBER

Autumn, I love thy parting look to view
    In cold November's day, so bleak and bare,
When thy life's dwindled thread worn nearly thro',
    With ling'ring, pott'ring pace, and head bleach'd bare,
Thou, like an old man, bidd'st the world adieu.
    I love thee well: and often, when a child,
Have roam'd the bare brown heath a flower to find;
    And in the moss-clad vale, and wood-bank wild,

Have cropt the little bell-flowers, paly blue,
    That trembling peept the shelt'ring bush behind.
When winnowing north-winds cold and blealy blew,
    How have I joy'd, with dithering hands, to find
Each fading flower; and still how sweet the blast,
Would bleak November's hour restore the joy that's past.

SUMMER MORNING

I LOVE to peep out on a summer's morn,
    Just as the scouting rabbit seeks her shed,
And the coy hare squats nestling in the corn,
    Frit at the bow'd ear tott'ring o'er her head;
And blund'ring pheasant, that from covert springs,
    His short sleep broke by early trampling feet,
Makes one to startle with his rustling wings,
    As through the boughs he seeks more safe retreat.
The little flower, begemm'd around with drops
    That shine at sunrise like to burnish'd gold,
'Tis sweet to view: the milk-maid often stops,
    And wonders much such spangles to behold;
The hedger, too, admires them deck the thorn,
And thinks he sees no beauties like the morn.

SABBATH WALKS

UPON the sabbath, sweet it is to walk
    'Neath wood-side shelter of oak's spreading tree,
Or by a hedgerow trace a padded balk,
    Or stretch 'neath willows on the meadow lea,
    List'ning, delighted, hum of passing bee,
And curious pausing on the blossom's head;
    And mark the spider at his labour free,
Spinning from bent to bent his silken thread,
    And lab'ring ants, by careful nature led
To make the most of summer's plenteous stay,
    And lady-cow, beneath its leafy shed,
Call'd, when I mix'd with children, 'clock-a-clay,'
    Pruning its red wings on its pleasing bed,
Glad like myself to shun the heat of day.

THE DRIVING BOY

THE driving boy, beside his team,
Of May-month's beauty now will dream,
And cock his hat, and turn his eye
On flower, and tree, and deepening sky;
And oft burst loud in fits of song,
And whistle as he reels along,
Cracking his whip in starts of joy—
A happy, dirty, driving boy.
The youth, who leaves his corner stool
Betimes for neighbouring village-school,
Where, as a mark to guide him right,
The church spire's all the way in sight,
With cheerings from his parents given,
Beneath the joyous smiles of heaven
Saunters, with many an idle stand,
With satchel swinging in his hand,
And gazes, as he passes by,
On everything that meets his eye.
Young lambs seem tempting him to play,
Dancing and bleating in his way;
With trembling tails and pointed ears
They follow him, and lose their fears;
He smiles upon their sunny faces,
And fain would join their happy races.
The birds, that sing on bush and tree,
Seem chirping for his company;
And all—in fancy's idle whim—
Seem keeping holiday, but him.
He lolls upon each resting stile,
To see the fields so sweetly smile,
To see the wheat grow green and long;
And lists the weeder's toiling song,
Or short note of the changing thrush
Above him in the whitethorn bush,
That o'er the leaning stile bends low
Its blooming mockery of snow.

THE INSECT WORLD

THE insect world amid the suns and dew
Awake and hum their tiny songs anew,
And climb the totter-grass and blossom's stem
As huge in size as mighty oaks to them;
And rushy burnets on the pasture rise
As tall as castles to their little eyes;
Each leaf's a town and the smooth meadow grass
A mighty world whose bounds they never pass;
E'en spots no bigger than the husbandman's
Or shepherd's noontide dwarf-shrunk shadow spans
—Or e'en the milkmaid tripping through the dew,
Each space she covers with her slender shoe—
Seem to their view high woods in which they roam
As lorn, lost wanderers many miles from home,
Creeping up bents and down whole weary hours
And resting oft on the soft breasts of flowers;
Till age, in minutes long as years, creeps on,
Or waning summer warns them to be gone.

FLOWERS

ERE yet the year is one month old,
  In spite of frost and wind and snow,
Bare-bosomed to the quaking cold,
  Spring's little selfsown flowers will blow;
And ever kin to early hours
  Peep aconites in cups of gold,
With frilled leaves muffled round their flowers
  Like tender maidens shunning cold;

And then as winter's parting pledge,
  Like true love in his crabbed reign,
The violets 'neath the naked hedge
  Peep thro' the rustling leaves again,
Soon as from off the thicket's moss
  The sunshine clears the doubting snow,
And the o'erjoyed and neighing horse
  Can find a patch of green to blow.

21

Like jewels brought by early hours,
   These little littered blossoms come;
Like wanderers from fairy bowers,
   They smile and gladly find a home;
And on the threshold of the spring,
   Like timid children out of doors,
They lie and wait the birds to sing,
   And laugh upon the splashy moors.

In April's smiling-frowning weather,
   Like younkers to a holiday,
The young flowers bud in troops together
   To wait the feast of merry May;
In sunny nooks and shelter nurst,
   Buds all their early blooms display,
Where sunbeams show their faces first
   And make when there the longest stay.

ENCLOSURE

FAR spread the moory ground, a level scene
Bespread with rush and one eternal green,
That never felt the rage of blundering plough,
Though centuries wreathed spring blossoms on its brow.
Autumn met plains that stretched them far away
In unchecked shadows of green, brown, and grey.
Unbounded freedom ruled the wandering scene;
No fence of ownership crept in between
To hide the prospect from the gazing eye;
Its only bondage was the circling sky.
A mighty flat, undwarfed by bush and tree,
Spread its faint shadow of immensity,
And lost itself, which seemed to eke its bounds,
In the blue mist the horizon's edge surrounds.

Now this sweet vision of my boyish hours,
Free as spring clouds and wild as forest flowers,
Is faded all—a hope that blossomed free,
And hath been once as it no more shall be.

Enclosure came, and trampled on the grave
Of labour's rights, and left the poor a slave;
And memory's pride, ere want to wealth did bow,
Is both the shadow and the substance now.
The sheep and cows were free to range as then
Where change might prompt, nor felt the bonds of men.
Cows went and came with every morn and night
To the wild pasture as their common right;
And sheep, unfolded with the rising sun,
Heard the swains shout and felt their freedom won,
Tracked the red fallow field and heath and plain,
Or sought the brook to drink, and roamed again;
While the glad shepherd traced their tracks along,
Free as the lark and happy as her song.
But now all's fled, and flats of many a dye
That seemed to lengthen with the following eye,
Moors losing from the sight, far, smooth, and blea,
Where swopt the plover in its pleasure free,
Are banished now with heaths once wild and gay
As poet's visions of life's early day.
Like mighty giants of their limbs bereft,
The skybound wastes in mangled garbs are left,
Fence meeting fence in owner's little bounds
Of field and meadow, large as garden-grounds,
In little parcels little minds to please,
With men and flocks imprisoned, ill at ease.
For with the poor scared freedom bade farewell,
And fortune-hunters totter where they fell;
They dreamed of riches in the rebel scheme
And find too truly that they did but dream.

TO ANNA, THREE YEARS OLD

My Anna, summer laughs in mirth,
    And we will of the party be,
And leave the crickets in the hearth
    For green fields' merry minstrelsy.

23

I see thee now with little hand
    Catch at each object passing by,
The happiest thing in all the land
    Except the bee and butterfly.

The weed-based arches' walls that stride
    O'er where the meadow water falls
Will turn thee from thy path aside
    To gaze upon the mossy walls.

And limpid brook that leaps along,
    Gilt with the summer's burnished gleam
Will stop thy little tale or song
    To gaze upon its crimping stream.

Thou'lt leave my hand with eager speed
    The new-discovered things to see—
The old pond with its water-weed
    And danger-daring willow-tree,
Who leans, an ancient invalid,
    O'er spots where deepest waters be.

In sudden shout and wild surprise
    I hear thy simple wonderment,
As new things meet thy childish eyes
    And wake some innocent intent ;

As bird or bee or butterfly
    Bounds through the crowd of merry leaves
And starts the rapture of thine eye
    To run for what it ne'er achieves;

The simple reasoning arguments
    Shaped to thy fancy's little view,
The joys and rapturous intents
    That everywhere pursue.

So dreamed I over hope's young boon,
    When merry summer was returning,
And little thought that time so soon
    Would change my early hope to mourning.

I thought to have heard thee mid the bowers
  To mock the cuckoo's merry song,
And see thee seek thy daisy flowers
  That's been thy anxious choice so long.

But thou art on the bed of pain,
  So tells each poor forsaken toy.
Ah, could I see that happy hour
  When these shall be thy heart's employ,
And see thee toddle o'er the plain,
  And stoop for flowers, and shout for joy.

THE PROGRESS OF RHYME

O SOUL-ENCHANTING poesy,
Thou'st long been all the world with me;
When poor, thy presence grows my wealth,
When sick, thy visions give me health,
When sad, thy sunny smile is joy
And was from e'en a tiny boy.
When trouble came, and toiling care
Seemed almost more than I could bear,
While threshing in the dusty barn
Or squashing in the ditch to earn
A pittance that would scarce allow
One joy to smooth my sweating brow
Where drop by drop would chase and fall,
Thy presence triumphed over all:
The vulgar they might frown and sneer,
Insult was mean but never near.
'Twas poesy's self that stopt the sigh
And malice met with no reply.
So was it in my earlier day
When sheep to corn had strayed away
Or horses closen gaps had broke,
Ere sunrise peeped or I awoke;
My master's frowns might force the tear,
But poesy came to check and cheer.
It glistened in my shamèd eye
But ere it fell the swoof was by.

I thought of luck in future days
When even he might find a praise.
I looked on poesy like a friend
To cheer me till my life should end.
'Twas like a parent's first regard
And love when beauty's voice was heard,
'Twas joy, 'twas hope, and maybe fear,
But still 'twas rapture everywhere.
My heart were ice unmoved to dwell,
Nor care for one I loved so well
Through rough and smooth, through good and ill,
That led me and attends me still.
Thou wert an early joy to me:
That joy was love and poesy;
And but for thee my idle lay
Had ne'er been urged in early day;
The harp imagination strung
Had ne'er been dreamed of; but among
The flowers in summer's fields of joy
I'd lain an idle rustic boy,
No hope to think of, fear or care,
And even love a stranger there.
But poesy that vision flung
Around me as I hummed and sung;
I glowered on beauty passing by,
Yet hardly turned my sheepish eye;
I worshipped, yet could hardly dare
To show I knew the goddess there,
Lest my presumptuous stare should gain
But frowns, ill humour, and disdain.
My first ambition was its praise,
My struggles aye in early days.
Had I by vulgar boldness torn
That hope when it was newly born,
By rudeness, gibes, and vulgar tongue,
The curse of the unfeeling throng,
Their scorn had frowned upon the lay
And hope and song had died away.
And I with nothing to atone
Had felt myself indeed alone.

But promises of days to come
The very fields would seem to hum,
Those burning days when I should dare
To sing aloud my worship there,
When beauty's self might turn its eye
Of praise: what could I do but try?
'Twas winter then, but summer shone
From heaven when I was all alone;
And summer came, and every weed
Of great or little had its meed;
Without its leaves there wa'n't a bower
Nor one poor weed without its flower.
'Twas love and pleasure all along;
I felt that I'd a right to song
And sung—but in a timid strain—
Of fondness for my native plain;
For everything I felt a love,
The weeds below, the birds above;
And weeds that bloomed in summer's hours
I thought they should be reckoned flowers;
They made a garden free for all,
And so I loved them great and small,
And sung of some that pleased my eye,
Nor could I pass the thistle by,
But paused and thought it could not be
A weed in nature's poesy.
No matter for protecting wall,
No matter though they chance to fall
Where sheep and cows and oxen lie,
The kindly rain when they're adry
Falls on them with as plenteous showers
As when it waters garden flowers;
They look up with a blushing eye
Upon a tender watching sky,
And still enjoy the kindling smile
Of sunshine though they live with toil,
As garden flowers with all their care,
For nature's love is ever there.
And so it cheered me while I lay
Among their beautiful array,

To think that I in humble dress
Might have a right to happiness
And sing as well as greater men;
And then I strung the lyre agen
And heartened up o'er toil and fear
And lived with rapture everywhere,
Till dayshine to my themes did come.
Just as a blossom bursts to bloom
And finds itself in thorny ways,
So did my musings meet with praise,
And though no garden care had I
My heart had love for poesy,
A simple love, a wild esteem,
As heartfelt as the linnet's dream
That mutters in its sleep at night
Some notes from ecstasy's delight.
Thus did I dream o'er joys and lie
Muttering dream-songs of poesy.
The night dislimned and waking day
Shook from wood leaves the drops away;
Hope came, storms calmed, and hue and cry
With her false pictures herded by,
With tales of help when help was not,
Of friends who urged to write or blot,
Whose taste were such that mine were shame
Had they not helped it into fame.
Poh! let the idle rumour ill,
Their vanity is never still;
My harp, though simple, was my own.
When I was in the fields alone
With none to help and none to hear
To bid me either hope or fear,
The bird or bee its chords would sound,
The air hummed melodies around;
I caught with eager ear the strain
And sung the music o'er again;
Or love or instinct flowing strong,
Fields were the essence of the song.
And fields and woods are still as mine,
Real teachers that are all divine;

So if my song be weak or tame
'Tis I, not they, who bear the blame;
But hope and cheer through good and ill,
They are my aids to worship still,
Still growing on a gentle tide
Nor foes could mar nor friends could guide;
Like pasture brooks through sun and shade,
Crooked as channels chance hath made,
It rambles as it loves to stray
And hope and feeling lead the way.
—Ay, birds, no matter what the tune,
Or 'croak' or 'tweet,' 'twas nature's boon
That brought them joy, and music flung
Its spell o'er every matin sung,
And e'en the sparrow's chirp to me
Was song in its felicity.
When grief hung o'er me like a cloud
Till hope seemed even in her shroud,
I whispered poesy's spell till they
Gleamed round me like a summer's day;
When tempests o'er my labours sung,
My soul to its responses rung,
And joined the chorus till the storm
Fell all unheeded, void of harm;
And each old leaning shielding tree
Were princely palaces to me,
Where I would sit me down and chime
My unheard rhapsodies to rhyme.
All I beheld of grand, with time
Grew up to beautiful's sublime:
The arching grove of ancient limes
That into roofs like churches climbs,
Grain intertwisting into grain,
That stops the sun and stops the rain
And spreads a gloom that never smiles,
Like ancient halls and minster aisles,
While all without a beauteous screen
Of summer's luscious leaves is seen,
While heard that everlasting hum
Of insects haunting where they bloom,

As though 'twas nature's very place
Of worship, where her mighty race
Of insect life and spirits too
In summer-time were wont to go,
Both insects and the breath of flowers,
To sing their maker's mighty powers.
I've thought so as I used to rove
Through Burghley Park, that darksome grove
Of limes where twilight lingered grey
Like evening in the midst of day.
I felt without a single skill
That instinct that would not be still,
To think of song sublime beneath
That heaved my bosom like my breath,
That burned and chilled and went and came
Without or uttering or a name,
Until the vision waked with time
And left me itching after rhyme,
Where little pictures idly tell
Of nature's powers and nature's spell.
I felt and shunned the idle vein,
Laid down the pen and toiled again;
But, spite of all, through good and ill,
It was and is my worship still.
No matter how the world approved,
'Twas nature listened, I that loved;
No matter how the lyre was strung,
From my own heart the music sprung.
The cowboy with his oaten straw,
Although he hardly heard or saw
No more of music than he made,
'Twas sweet; and when I pluckt the blade
Of grass upon the woodland hill
To mock the birds with artless skill,
No music in the world beside
Seemed half so sweet, till mine was tried.
So my boy-worship poesy
Made e'en the muses pleased with me,
Until I even danced for joy,
A happy and a lonely boy,

Each object to my ear and eye
Made paradise of poesy.
I heard the blackbird in the dell
Sing sweet; could I but sing as well,
I thought, until the bird in glee
Seemed pleased and paused to answer me.
And nightingales—Oh, I have stood
Beside the pingle and the wood,
And o'er the old oak railing hung
To listen every note they sung,
And left boys making taws of clay
To music and listen half the day.
The more I listened and the more
Each note seemed sweeter than before,
And aye so different was the strain
She'd scarce repeat the note again:
'Chew-chew chew-chew,' and higher still:
'Cheer-cheer cheer-cheer,' more loud and shrill:
'Cheer-up cheer-up cheer-up,' and dropt
Low: 'tweet tweet jug jug jug,' and stopt
One moment just to drink the sound
Her music made, and then a round
Of stranger witching notes was heard,
As if it was a stranger bird:
'Wew-wew wew-wew, chur-chur chur-chur,
Woo-it woo-it': could this be her?
'Tee-rew tee-rew tee-rew tee-rew,
Chew-rit chew-rit,' and ever new:
'Will-will will-will, grig-grig grig-grig.'
The boy stopt sudden on the brig
To hear the 'tweet tweet tweet' so shrill,
Then 'jug jug jug,' and all was still
A minute, when a wilder strain
Made boys and woods to pause again;
Words were not left to hum the spell.
Could they be birds that sung so well?
I thought, and maybe more than I,
That music's self had left the sky
To cheer me with its magic strain;
And then I hummed the words again,

31

Till fancy pictured, standing by,
My heart's companion, poesy.
No friends had I to guide or aid
The struggles young ambition made.
In silent shame the harp was tried
And rapture's griefs the tune applied,
Yet o'er the songs my parents sung
My ear in silent musings hung.
Their kindness wishes did regard,
They sung, and joy was my reward.
All else was but a proud decree,
The right of bards and naught to me,
A title that I dared not claim
And hid it like a private shame.
I whispered aye and felt a fear
To speak aloud though none was near;
I dreaded laughter more than blame,
I dared not sing aloud for shame;
So all unheeded, lone and free,
I felt it happiness to be
Unknown, obscure, and like a tree
In woodland peace and privacy.
No, not a friend on earth had I
But my own kin and poesy,
Nor wealth, and yet I felt indeed
As rich as anybody need
To be, for health and hope and joy
Was mine, although a lonely boy,
And what I felt, as now I sing,
Made friends of all and everything
Save man the vulgar and the low;
The polished 'twas not mine to know
Who paid me in my after days
And gave me even more than praise:
'Twas then I found that friends indeed
Were needed when I'd less to need.
The pea, that independent springs,
When in its blossom, trails and clings
To every help that lingers by,
And I, when classed with poesy,

32

Who stood unbrunt the heaviest shower,
Felt feeble as that very flower
And helpless all; but beauty's smile
Is harvest for the hardest toil,
Whose smiles I little thought to win
With ragged coat and downy chin,
A clownish, silent, aguish boy
Who even felt ashamed of joy,
So dirty, ragged, and so low,
With naught to recommend or show
That I was worthy e'en a smile.
Had I but felt amid my toil
That I in days to come should be
A little light in minstrelsy,
And in the blush of after days
Win beauty's smile and beauty's praise,
My heart with lonely fancy warm
Had even bursted with the charm;
And Mary, thou whose very name
I loved, whose look was even fame,
From those delicious eyes of blue
In smiles and rapture ever new,
Thy timid step, thy fairy form,
Thy face with blushes ever warm,
When praise my schoolboy heart did move;
I saw thy blush and thought it love.
And all ambitious thee to please
My heart was ever ill at ease;
I saw thy beauty grow with days,
And tried song-pictures in thy praise,
And all of fair or beautiful
Were thine akin, nor could I pull
The blossoms that I thought divine
Lest I should injure aught of thine.
So where they grew I let them be,
And though I dare not talk to thee
Of love, to them I talked aloud,
And grew ambitious from the crowd
With hopes that I one day should be
Beloved, Mary, e'en by thee.

33

But I mistook in early day
The world, and so our hopes decay
Yet that same cheer in after toils
Was poesy, and still she smiles
As sweet as blossoms to the tree,
And hope, love, joy, are poesy.

TO THE RURAL MUSE

Muse of the fields, oft have I said farewell
To thee, my boon companion, loved so long
And hung thy sweet harp in the bushy dell,
For abler hands to wake an abler song.
Much did I fear my homage did thee wrong:
Yet, loath to leave, as oft I turned again;
And to its wires mine idle hands would cling,
Torturing it into song. It may be vain;
Yet still I try, ere fancy droops her wing,
And hopeless silence comes to numb its every string.

Muse of the pasture brooks, on thy calm sea
Of poesy I've sailed; and though the will
To speed were greater than my prowess be,
I've ventured with much fear of usage ill,
Yet more of joy. Though timid be my skill,
As not to dare the depths of mightier streams,
Yet rocks abide in shallow ways, and I
Have much of fear to mingle with my dreams.
Yet, lovely muse, I still believe thee by,
And think I see thee smile, and so forget I sigh.

Muse of the cottage hearth, oft did I tell
My hopes to thee, nor feared to plead in vain;
But felt around my heart thy witching spell,
That bade me as thy worshipper remain:
I did so, and still worship. Oh! again
Smile on my offerings, and so keep them green;
Bedeck my fancies like the clouds of even,
Mingling all hues which thou from heaven dost glean.
To me a portion of thy power be given,
If theme so mean as mine may merit aught of heaven.

34

Still, sweet enchantress, youth's strong feelings move,
That from thy presence their existence took:
The innocent idolatry and love,
Paying thee worship in each secret nook,
That fancied friends in tree, and flower, and brook,
Shaped clouds to angels and beheld them smile,
And heard commending tongues in every wind.
Life's grosser fancies did these dreams defile,
Yet not entirely root them from the mind;
I think I hear them still, and often look behind.

Ay, I have heard thee in the summer wind,
As if commending what I sung to thee;
Ay, I have seen thee on a cloud reclined,
Kindling my fancies into poesy;
I saw thee smile, and took the praise to me.
In beauties, past all beauty, thou wert drest;
I thought the very clouds around thee knelt:
I saw the sun to linger in the west,
Paying thee worship; and as eve did melt
In dews, they seemed thy tears for sorrows I had felt.

SUDDEN SHOWER

BLACK grows the southern sky, betokening rain,
    And humming hive-bees homeward hurry by:
They feel the change; so let us shun the grain,
    And take the broad road while our feet are dry.
Ay, there some dropples moistened on my face,
    And pattered on my hat—'tis coming nigh!
Let's look about, and find a sheltering place.
    The little things around, like you and I,
Are hurrying through the grass to shun the shower.
    Here stoops an ash-tree—hark! the wind gets high,
But never mind; this ivy, for an hour,
    Rain as it may, will keep us dryly here:
That little wren knows well his sheltering bower,
    Nor leaves his dry house though we come so near.

HOME PICTURES IN MAY

THE sunshine bathes in clouds of many hues
And morning's feet are gemmed with early dews;
Warm daffodils about the garden beds
Peep through their pale slim leaves their golden heads,
Sweet earthly suns of spring; the gosling broods,
In coats of sunny green, about the road
Waddle in ecstasy; and in rich moods
The old hen leads her flickering chicks abroad
Oft scuttling 'neath her wings to see the kite
Hang wavering o'er them in the spring's blue light.
The sparrows round their new nests chirp with glee
And sweet the robin spring's young luxury shares,
Tootling its song in feathery gooseberry tree
While watching worms the gardener's spade unbares.

THE WRYNECK'S NEST

THAT summer bird its oft-repeated note
   Chirps from the dotterel ash, and in the hole
The green woodpecker made in years remote,
   It makes its nest. When peeping idlers stroll
In anxious plundering moods, they by and by
   The wryneck's curious eggs, as white as snow,
While squinting in the hollow tree, espy.
The sitting bird looks up with jetty eye,
   And waves her head in terror to and fro,
Speckled and veined with various shades of brown;
And then a hissing noise assails the clown.
   Quickly, with hasty terror in his breast,
From the tree's knotty trunk he sluthers down,
   And thinks the strange bird guards a serpent's nest.

THE LADY-FLY

TENANT of leaves and flowers and glossy stalks,
   The wild profusion that the summer brings,
Hiding in crowding beans and benty baulks,
   Where, on the knapweed while the cricket sings

I often watch thee prune thy speckled wings,
On the smooth stem advancing yet more high,
Till with the help the puffing zephyr brings
Thou'lt stretch thy finer wings of gauze and fly,
In changing scenes more snug and cool to lie.
Ah, when a cow-boy I at ease reclined
Upon a thymy hill, and thou wert nigh,
What fond inquiries filled my curious mind!
How have I watched thy pastimes, lady-fly,
And thought thee happiest creature of thy kind!

MAY

Birds sing and build, and Nature scorns alone
On May's young festival to keep a widow;
The children too have pleasures all their own,
A-plucking lady-smocks along the meadow.
The little brook sings loud among the pebbles,
So very loud that water-flowers, which lie
Where many a silver curdle boils and dribbles,
Dance too with joy as it goes singing by.
Among the pasture mole-hills maidens stoop
To pluck the luscious marjoram for their bosoms;
The greensward's smothered o'er with buttercups,
And whitethorns, they are breaking down with blossoms!
'Tis Nature's livery for the bonny May,
Who keeps her court, and all have holiday.

THE WOODMAN

Now evening comes, and from the new-laid hedge
The woodman rustles in his leathern guise,
Hiding in ditches lined with bristling sedge
His bill and mittens from theft's meddling eyes,
Within his wallet storing many a pledge
Of flowers and boughs from early-sprouting trees.
And painted pooties from the ivied hedge,
About its mossy roots—his boys to please,
Who wait with merry joy his coming home,
Anticipating presents such as these

Gained far afield, where they, or night or morn,
   Find no school leisure long enough to go,
Where flowers but rarely from their stalks are torn,
   And birds scarce lose a nest the season through.

AUTUMN

SIREN of sullen moods and fading hues,
Yet haply not incapable of joy,
      Sweet Autumn! I thee hail
      With welcome all unfeigned;

And oft as morning from her lattice peeps
To beckon up the sun, I seek with thee
      To drink the dewy breath
      Of fields left fragrant then,

In solitudes, where no frequented paths
But what thy own foot makes betray thy home,
      Stealing obtrusive there
      To meditate thy end:

By overshadowed ponds, in woody nooks,
With ramping sallows lined, and crowding sedge,
      Which woo the winds to play,
      And with them dance for joy;

And meadow pools, torn wide by lawless floods,
Where water-lilies spread their oily leaves,
      On which, as wont, the fly
      Oft battens in the sun;

Where leans the mossy willow half-way o'er,
On which the shepherd crawls astride to throw
      His angle clear of weeds
      That crowd the water's brim;

Or crispy hills, and hollows scant of sward,
Where step by step the patient lonely boy
      Hath cut rude flights of stairs
      To climb their steepy sides;

Then track along their feet, grown hoarse with noise,
The crawling brook, that ekes its weary speed,
    And struggles through the weeds
    With faint and sullen brawl.

These haunts I long have favoured, more as now
With thee thus wandering, moralizing on,
    Stealing glad thoughts from grief,
    And happy, though I sigh.

Sweet Vision, with the wild dishevelled hair,
And raiment shadowy of each wind's embrace,
    Fain would I win thine harp
    To one accordant theme;

Now not inaptly craved, communing thus
Beneath the curdled arms of this stunt oak,
    While pillowed on the grass,
    We fondly ruminate

O'er the disordered scenes of woods and fields,
Ploughed lands, thin travelled with half-hungry sheep,
    Pastures tracked deep with cows,
    Where small birds seek for seed:

Marking the cow-boy that so merry trills
His frequent, unpremeditated song,
    Wooing the winds to pause,
    Till echo brawls again;

As on with plashy step and clouted shoon
He roves, half indolent and self-employed,
    To rob the little birds
    Of hips and pendent haws,

And sloes, dim covered as with dewy veils,
And rambling bramble-berries, pulp and sweet,
    Arching their prickly trails
    Half o'er the narrow lane:

Noting the hedger front with stubborn face
The dank blea wind, that whistles thinly by
    His leathern garb, thorn-proof,
    And cheek red-hot with toil.

While o'er the pleachy lands of mellow brown,
The mower's stubbling scythe clogs to his foot
    The ever eking wisp,
    With sharp and sudden jerk,

Till into formal rows the russet shocks
Crowd the blank field to thatch time-weathered barns,
    And hovels rude repair,
    Stript by disturbing winds.

See! from the rustling scythe the haunted hare
Scampers circuitous, with startled ears
    Prickt up, then squat, as by
    She brushes to the woods,

Where reeded grass, breast-high and undisturbed,
Forms pleasant clumps, through which the soothing winds
    Soften her rigid fears,
    And lull to calm repose.

Wild sorceress! me thy restless mood delights
More than the stir of summer's crowded scenes,
    Where, jostled in the din,
    Joy palled my ear with song;

Heart-sickening for the silence that is thine,
Not broken inharmoniously, as now
    That lone and vagrant bee
    Booms faint with weary chime.

Now filtering winds thin winnow through the woods
In tremulous noise, that bids, at every breath,
    Some sickly cankered leaf
    Let go its hold, and die.

And now the bickering storm, with sudden start,
In flirting fits of anger carps aloud,
    Thee urging to thine end,
    Sore wept by troubled skies.

And yet, sublime in grief, thy thoughts delight
To show me visions of most gorgeous dyes,
    Haply forgetting now
    They but prepare thy shroud;

Thy pencil dashing its excess of shades,
Improvident of waste, till every bough
    Burns with thy mellow touch
    Disorderly divine.

Soon must I view thee as a pleasant dream
Droop faintly, and so sicken for thine end,
    As sad the winds sink low
    In dirges for their queen;

While in the moment of their weary pause,
To cheer thy bankrupt pomp, the willing lark
    Starts from his shielding clod,
    Snatching sweet scraps of song.

Thy life is waning now, and silence tries
To mourn, but meets no sympathy in sounds,
    As stooping low she bends,
    Forming with leaves thy grave;

To sleep inglorious there mid tangled woods,
Till parch-lipped summer pines in drought away,
    Then from thine ivied trance
    Awake to glories new.

SUMMER IMAGES

I LOVE at early morn, from new-mown swath,
   To see the startled frog his route pursue,
And mark while, leaping o'er the dripping path,
   His bright sides scatter dew;
And early lark that from its bustle flies
   To hail his matin new;
      And watch him to the skies:

And note on hedgerow baulks, in moisture sprent,
   The jetty snail creep from the mossy thorn,
With earnest heed and tremulous intent,
   Frail brother of the morn,
That from the tiny bents and misted leaves
   Withdraws his timid horn,
      And fearful vision weaves:

Or swallow heed on smoke-tanned chimney-top,
   Wont to be first unsealing morning's eye,
Ere yet the bee hath gleaned one wayward drop
   Of honey on his thigh;
To see him seek morn's airy couch to sing,
   Until the golden sky
      Bepaint his russet wing:

And sawning boy by tanning corn espy,
   With clapping noise to startle birds away,
And hear him bawl to every passer-by
   To know the hour of day;
And see the uncradled breeze, refreshed and strong,
   With waking blossoms play,
      And breathe aeolian song.

I love the south-west wind, or low or loud,
   And not the less when sudden drops of rain
Moisten my pallid cheek from ebon cloud,
   Threatening soft showers again,
That over lands new ploughed and meadow grounds,
Summer's sweet breath unchain,
      And wake harmonious sounds.

Rich music breathes in summer's every sound;
  And in her harmony of varied greens,
Woods, meadows, hedgerows, cornfields, all around
  Much beauty intervenes,
Filling with harmony the ear and eye;
  While o'er the mingling scenes
    Far spreads the laughing sky.

And wind-enamoured aspen—mark the leaves
  Turn up their silver lining to the sun,
And list! the brustling noise, that oft deceives,
  And makes the sheep-boy run:
The sound so mimics fast-approaching showers,
  He thinks the rain begun,
    And hastes to sheltering bowers.

THE ETERNITY OF NATURE

LEAVES from eternity are simple things
To the world's gaze—whereto a spirit clings
Sublime and lasting. Trampled under foot,
The daisy lives, and strikes its little root
Into the lap of time: centuries may come,
And pass away into the silent tomb,
And still the child, hid in the womb of time,
Shall smile and pluck them when this simple rhyme
Shall be forgotten, like a churchyard stone,
Or lingering lie unnoticed and alone.
When eighteen hundred years, our common date,
Grow many thousands in their marching state,
Ay, still the child, with pleasure in his eye,
Shall cry—the daisy! a familiar cry—
And run to pluck it, in the self-same state
As when Time found it in his infant date;
And, like a child himself, when all was new,
Might smile with wonder, and take notice too.
Its little golden bosom, frilled with snow,
Might win e'en Eve to stoop adown, and show
Her partner, Adam, in the silky grass
This little gem that smiled where pleasure was,

And loving Eve, from Eden followed ill,
And bloomed with sorrow, and lives smiling still,
As once in Eden under heaven's breath,
So now on earth, and on the lap of death
It smiles for ever.—Cowslips of gold bloom,
That in the pasture and the meadow come,
Shall come when kings and empires fade and die;
And in the closen, as Time's partners, lie
As fresh two thousand years to come as now,
With those five crimson spots upon their brow.
The little brooks that hum a simple lay
In green unnoticed spots, from praise away,
Shall sing when poets in time's darkness hid
Shall lie like memory in a pyramid,
Forgetting yet not all forgot, though lost
Like a thread's end in ravelled windings crost.
The little humble-bee shall hum as long
As nightingales, for Time protects the song;
And Nature is their soul, to whom all clings
Of fair or beautiful in lasting things.
The little robin in the quiet glen,
Hidden from fame and all the strife of men,
Sings unto Time a pastoral, and gives
A music that lives on and ever lives.
Spring and autumnal years shall bloom, and fade,
Longer than songs that poets ever made.
Think ye not these, Time's playthings, pass proud skill?
Time loves them like a child, and ever will;
And so I seek them in each bushy spot,
And sing with them when all else notice not,
And feel the music of their mirth agree
With that sooth quiet that bestirs in me.
And if I touch aright that quiet tone,
That soothing truth that shadows forth their own,
Then many a year to come, in after-days,
Shall still find hearts to love my quiet lays.
Thus cheering mirth with thoughts sung not for fame,
But for the joy that with their utterance came,
That inward breath of rapture urged not loud—
Birds, singing lone, fly silent past a crowd—

In these same pastoral spots, which childish time
Makes dear to me, I wander out and rhyme;
What hour the dewy morning's infancy
Hangs on each blade of grass and every tree,
And sprents the red thighs of the humble-bee,
Who 'gins betimes unwearied minstrelsy;
Who breakfasts, dines, and most divinely sups,
With every flower save golden buttercups—
On whose proud bosoms he will never go,
But passes by with scarcely, 'How do ye do?'
Since in their showy, shining, gaudy cells
Haply the summer's honey never dwells.
All nature's ways are mysteries! Endless youth
Lives in them all, unchangeable as truth.
With the odd number five, her curious laws
Play many freaks, nor once mistake the cause;
For in the cowslip-peeps this very day
Five spots appear, which Time wears not away,
Nor once mistakes in counting—look within
Each peep, and five, nor more nor less, are seen.
So trailing bindweed, with its pinky cup,
Five leaves of paler hue go streaking up;
And many a bird, too, keeps the rule alive,
Laying five eggs, nor more nor less than five.
But flowers, how many own that mystic power,
With five leaves ever making up the flower!
The five-leaved grass, mantling its golden cup
Of flowers—five leaves make all for which I stoop.
The bryony, in the hedge, that now adorns
The tree to which it clings, and now the thorns,
Owns five-starred pointed leaves of dingy white;
Count which I will, all make the number right.
The spreading goose-grass, trailing all abroad
In leaves of silver green about the road—
Five leaves make every blossom all along.
I stoop for many, none are counted wrong.
'Tis Nature's wonder, and her Maker's will,
Who bade earth be, and order owns him still,
As that superior Power, who keeps the key
Of wisdom and of might through all eternity.

PASTORAL FANCIES

Sweet pastime here my mind so entertains,
  Abiding pleasaunce and heart-feeding joys,
To meet this blithesome day, these painted plains,
  Those singing maids and chubby laughing boys,
  Which hay-time and the summer here employs—
My rod and line doth all neglected lie;
  A higher joy my former sport destroys:
Nature this day doth bait the hook, and I
The glad fish am, that's to be caught thereby.

This silken grass, these pleasant flowers in bloom,
  Among these tasty mole-hills that do lie
Like summer cushions for all guests that come,
  Those little feathered folk, that sing and fly
  Above these trees, in that so gentle sky,
Where not a cloud dares soil its heavenly light,
  And this smooth river softly grieving by—
All fill mine eyes with so divine a sight
As makes me sigh that it should e'er be night.

In sooth, methinks the choice I most should prize
  Were in these meadows of delight to dwell,
To share the joyaunce heaven elsewhere denies,
  The calmness that doth relish passing well
  The quiet conscience, that aye bears the bell,
And happy musings nature would supply,
  Leaving no room for troubles to rebel:
Here would I think all day, at night would lie,
The hay my bed, my coverlid the sky.

So would I live as nature might command,
  Taking with providence my wholesome meals;
Plucking the savoury peascod from the land,
  Where rustic lad oft dainty dinner steals.
  For drink, I'd hie me where the moss conceals
The little spring so chary from the sun,
  Then lie, and listen to the merry peals
Of distant bells—all other noises shun;
Then court the muses till the day be done.

46

Here would high joys my lowly choice requite;
  For garden plot, I'd choose this flowery lea;
Here I in culling nosegays would delight,
  The lambtoe tuft, the paler culverkey:
  The cricket's mirth were talk enough for me
When talk I needed; and when warmed to pray,
  The little birds my choristers should be,
Who wear one suit for worship and for play
And make the whole year round one sabbath-day.

A thymy hill should be my cushioned seat;
  An aged thorn, with wild hops intertwined,
My bower, where I from noontide might retreat;
  A hollow oak would shield me from the wind,
  Or, as might hap, I better shed could find
In gentle spot, where fewer paths intrude,
  The hut of shepherd swain, with rushes lined:
There would I tenant be to Solitude,
Seeking life's gentlest joys, to shun the rude;

Bidding a long farewell to every trouble,
  The envy and the hate of evil men;
Feeling cares lessen, happiness redouble,
  And all I lost as if 'twere found agen.
  Vain life unseen; the past alone known then:
No worldly intercourse my mind should have,
  To lure me backward to its crowded den;
Here would I live and die, and only crave
The home I chose might also be my grave.

INSECTS

THESE tiny loiterers on the barley's beard,
And happy units of a numerous herd
Of playfellows, the laughing summer brings,
Mocking the sunshine in their glittering wings,
How merrily they creep, and run, and fly!
No kin they bear to labour's drudgery,

Smoothing the velvet of the pale hedge-rose;
And where they fly for dinner no one knows—
The dew-drops feed them not—they love the shine
Of noon, whose sun may bring them golden wine.
All day they're playing in their Sunday dress—
Till night goes sleep, and they can do no less;
Then, to the heath-bell's silken hood they fly,
And like to princes in their slumbers lie,
Secure from night, and dropping dews, and all,
In silken beds and roomy painted hall.
So merrily they spend their summer day,
Now in the cornfields, now the new-mown hay,
One almost fancies that such happy things,
With coloured hoods and richly burnished wings,
Are fairy folk, in splendid masquerade
Disguised, as if of mortal folk afraid,
Keeping their merry pranks a mystery still,
Lest glaring day should do their secrets ill.

WILD BEES

THESE children of the sun which summer brings
As pastoral minstrels in her merry train
Pipe rustic ballads upon busy wings
And glad the cotters' quiet toils again.
The white-nosed bee that bores its little hole
In mortared walls and pipes its symphonies,
And never absent cousin, black as coal,
That Indian-like bepaints its little thighs,
With white and red bedight for holiday,
Right earlily a-morn do pipe and play
And with their legs stroke slumber from their eyes;
And aye so fond they of their singing seem
That in their holes abed at close of day
They still keep piping in their honey dreams;
And larger ones that thrum on ruder pipe
Round the sweet-smelling closen and rich woods,
Where tawny white and red-flusht clover buds
Shine bonnily, and bean-fields, blossom-ripe,
Shed dainty perfumes and give honey food

To these sweet poets of the summer fields;
Me much delighting as I stroll along
The narrow path that hay-laid meadow yields,
Catching the windings of their wandering song.
The black and yellow bumble, first on wing
To buzz among the sallow's early flowers,
Hiding its nest in holes from fickle spring
Who stints his rambles with her frequent showers;
And one that may for wiser piper pass,
In livery dress half sables and half red,
Who laps a moss-ball in the meadow grass
And hoards her stores when April showers have fled;
And russet commoner who knows the face
Of every blossom that the meadow brings,
Starting the traveller to a quicker pace
By threatening round his head in many rings:
These sweeten summer in their happy glee
By giving for her honey melody.

THE FALLEN ELM

OLD elm, that murmured in our chimney-top
The sweetest anthem autumn ever made
And into mellow whispering calms would drop
When showers fell on thy many-coloured shade
And when dark tempests mimic thunder made—
While darkness came as it would strangle light
With the black tempest of a winter night
That rocked thee like a cradle in thy root—
How did I love to hear the winds upbraid
Thy strength without—while all within was mute.
It seasoned comfort to our hearts' desire,
We felt thy kind protection like a friend
And edged our chairs up closer to the fire,
Enjoying comfort that was never penned.
Old favourite tree, thou'st seen time's changes lower,
Though change till now did never injure thee;
For time beheld thee as her sacred dower
And nature claimed thee her domestic tree.

Storms came and shook thee many a weary hour,
Yet steadfast to thy home thy roots have been;
Summers of thirst parched round thy homely bower
Till earth grew iron—still thy leaves were green.
The children sought thee in thy summer shade
And made their playhouse rings of stick and stone;
The mavis sang and felt himself alone
While in thy leaves his early nest was made,
And I did feel his happiness mine own,
Naught heeding that our friendship was betrayed,
Friend not inanimate—though stocks and stones
There are, and many formed of flesh and bones.
Thou owned a language by which hearts are stirred
Deeper than by a feeling clothed in word,
And speakest now what's known of every tongue,
Language of pity and the force of wrong.
What cant assumes, what hypocrites will dare,
Speaks home to truth and shows it what they are.
I see a picture which thy fate displays
And learn a lesson from thy destiny;
Self-interest saw thee stand in freedom's ways—
So thy old shadow must a tyrant be.
Thou'st heard the knave, abusing those in power,
Bawl freedom loud and then oppress the free;
Thou'st sheltered hypocrites in many a shower,
That when in power would never shelter thee.
Thou'st heard the knave supply his canting powers
With wrong's illusions when he wanted friends;
That bawled for shelter when he lived in showers
And when clouds vanished made thy shade amends—
With axe at root he felled thee to the ground
And barked of freedom—Oh, I hate the sound.
Time hears its visions speak, and age sublime
Hath made thee a disciple unto time.
—It grows the cant term of enslaving tools
To wrong another by the name of right;
It grows the licence of o'erbearing fools
To cheat plain honesty by force of might.
Thus came enclosure—ruin was its guide,
But freedom's clapping hands enjoyed the sight

Though comfort's cottage soon was thrust aside[1]
And workhouse prisons raised upon the site.
E'en nature's dwellings far away from men,
The common heath, became the spoiler's prey;
The rabbit had not where to make his den,
And labour's only cow was drove away.
No matter—wrong was right and right was wrong,
And freedom's bawl was sanction to the song.
—Such was thy ruin, music-making elm;
The right of freedom was to injure thine:
As thou wert served, so would they overwhelm
In freedom's name the little that is mine.
And there are knaves that brawl for better laws
And cant of tyranny in stronger power,
Who glut their vile unsatiated maws
And freedom's birthright from the weak devour.

SPORT IN THE MEADOWS

MAYTIME is to the meadows coming in,
And cowslip peeps have gotten e'er so big,
And water-blobs and all their golden kin
Crowd round the shallows by the striding brig.
Daisies and buttercups and lady-smocks
Are all abouten shining here and there,
Nodding about their gold and yellow locks
Like morts of folken flocking at a fair.
The sheep and cows are crowding for a share
And snatch the blossoms in such eager haste
That basket-bearing children running there
Do think within their hearts they'll get them all
And hoot and drive them from their graceless waste
As though there wa'n't a cowslip peep to spare.
—For they want some for tea and some for wine
And some to maken up a cuckaball
To throw across the garland's silken line
That reaches o'er the street from wall to wall.
—Good gracious me, how merrily they fare!

[1] Preceding five lines restored from MS.

51

One sees a fairer cowslip than the rest,
And off they shout—the foremost bidding fair
To get the prize—and earnest half and jest
The next one pops her down—and from her hand
Her basket falls and out her cowslips all
Tumble and litter there—the merry band
In laughing friendship round about her fall
To helpen gather up the littered flowers
That she no loss may mourn. And now the wind,
In frolic mood among the merry hours,
Wakens with sudden start and tosses off
Some untied bonnet on its dancing wings;
Away they follow with a scream and laugh,
And aye the youngest ever lags behind,
Till on the deep lake's very brink it hings.
They shout and catch it and then off they start
And chase for cowslips merry as before,
And each one seems so anxious at the heart
As they would even get them all and more.
One climbs a mole-hill for a bunch of may,
One stands on tiptoe for a linnet's nest
And pricks her hand and throws her flowers away
And runs for plantain leaves to have it drest.
So do they run abouten all the day
And tease the grass-hid larks from getting rest.
—Scarce give they time in their unruly haste
To tie a shoestring that the grass unties—
And thus they run the meadows' bloom to waste,
Till even comes and dulls their phantasies,
When one finds losses out to stifle smiles
Of silken bonnet-strings—and utters sigh
O'er garments renten clambering over stiles.
Yet in the morning fresh afield they hie,
Bidding the last day's troubles all good-bye;
When red pied cow again their coming hears,
And ere they clap the gate she tosses up
Her head and hastens from the sport she fears:
The old yoe calls her lamb, nor cares to stoop
To crop a cowslip in their company.
Thus merrily the little noisy troop

Along the grass as rude marauders hie,
For ever noisy and for ever gay
While keeping in the meadows holiday.

THE SUMMER SHOWER

I love it well, o'ercanopied in leaves
    Of crowding woods, to spend a quiet hour,
And where the woodbine weaves
    To list the summer shower

Brought by the south-west wind, that balm and bland
    Breathes luscious coolness, loved and felt by all,
While on the uplifted hand
    The rain-drops gently fall;

Now quickening on and on, the pattering wood
    Receives the coming shower; birds trim their wings,
And in a joyful mood
    The little woodchat sings;

And blackbird, squatting in her mortared nest
    Safe hid in ivy and the pathless wood,
Pruneth her sooty breast
    And warms her downy brood;

And little pettichap, like hurrying mouse,
    Keeps nimbling near my arbour round and round;
Ay, there's her oven house,
    Built nearly on the ground

Of woodbents, withered straws, and moss, and leaves,
    And lined with downy feathers; safety's joy
Dwells with the home she weaves,
    Nor fears the pilfering boy.

The busy falling rain increases now,
    And sopping leaves their dripping moisture pour,
And from each loaded bough
    Fast falls the double shower.

Weeds, climbing hedges, banks, and meads unmown,
  Where rushy-fringèd brooklet easy curls,
Look joyous while the rain
  Strings their green suit with pearls;

While from the crouching corn the weeding troop
  Run hastily, and huddling in a ring
Where the old willows stoop,
  Their ancient ballads sing

And gabble over wonder's ceaseless tale,
  Till from the south-west sky showers thicker come,
Humming along the vale,
  And bid them hasten home.

With laughing skip they stride the hasty brook
  That mutters through the weeds until it gain
A clear and quiet nook
  To greet the dimpling rain;

And on they drabble all, in mirth not mute,
  Leaving their footmarks on the elting soil
Where print of sprawling foot
  Stirs up a tittering smile

On beauty's lips, who, slipping mid the crowd,
  Blushes to have her ankle seen so high,
Yet inly feeleth proud
  That none a fault can spy.

Yet rudely followed by the meddling clown
  Who passes vulgar gibes, the bashful maid
Lets go her folded gown
  And pauses half afraid

To climb the stile before him, till the dame,
  To quarrel half provoked, assails the knave
And laughs him into shame
  And makes him well behave.

Bird-nesting boys, o'ertaken in the rain,
　Beneath the ivied maple bustling run
And wait in anxious pain,
　Impatient for the sun,

And sigh for home; yet at the pasture gate,
　The molehill-tossing bull with straining eye
Seemeth their steps to wait
　Nor dare they pass him by;

Till, wearied out, high over hedge they scrawl
　To shun the road and through the wet grass roam,
Till wet and daggled all
　They fear to venture home.

The plough team wet and dripping plashes home,
　And on the horse the ploughboy lolls along,
Yet from the wet grounds come
　The loud and merry song.

Now 'neath the leafy arch of dripping bough
　That loaded trees form o'er the narrow lane,
The horse released from plough
　Naps the moist grass again.

Around their blanket camps the gipsies still,
　Heedless of showers while blackthorns shelter round
Jump o'er the pasture hill
　In many an idle bound.

From dark green clumps among the dripping grain
　The lark with sudden impulse starts and sings,
And mid the smoking rain
　Quivers her russet wings.

Amid the yellow furze, the rabbits' bed,
　Labour hath hid his tools and o'er the heath
Hies to the milking shed
　That stands the oak beneath;

And there he whiles the pleasant shower away,
    Filling his mind with store of happy things,
Rich crops of corn and hay
    And all that plenty brings.

The crampt horizon now leans on the ground
    Quiet and cool, and labour's hard employ
Ceases, while all around
    Falls a refreshing joy.

FAIRY THINGS

GREY lichens, mid thy hills of creeping thyme,
Grow like to fairy forests hung with rime;
And fairy money-pots are often found
That spring like little mushrooms out of ground,
Some shaped like cups and some in slender trim
Wineglasses like, that to the very rim
Are filled with little mystic shining seed;
We thought our fortunes promising indeed,
Expecting by and by ere night to find
Money ploughed up of more substantial kind.

Acres of little yellow weeds,
The wheat-field's constant blooms,
That ripen into prickly seeds
For fairy curry-combs,
To comb and clean the little things
That draw their nightly wain;
And so they scrub the beetle's wings
Till he can fly again.

And flannel felt for the beds of the queen
From the soft inside of the shell of the bean,
Where the gipsies down in the lonely dells
Had littered and left the plundered shells.

FRAGMENTS

The daisy wan, the primrose pale,
　Seem naught but white and yellow flowers
To every heedless passer-by,
　When they attend the spring's young hours;
But they are loves and friends to me,
　That tell me in each short sojourn
Of what they felt and I did feel
　In springs that never will return.

Envy and hatred from the world's rude pack
Follow success in almost every track,
Like lurking winters that are sure to bring
Storms to discomfort the young green of spring,
Crispt brown and icicled o'er with frosty chill;
But spring gets green at last as poesy will.

EXPECTATION: A BALLAD

'Tis Saturday night, and my shepherd will come
　With a hallo and whistle for me;
Be clear, O ye skies, take your storm-burthens home,
　Let no rain drench our favourite tree.
For I fear by the things that are hopping about
　There's a sign of a storm coming on;
The frog looks as black as the toad that creeps out
　From under its hiding-stone.

The cat with her tail runneth round till she reels
　And the pigs race with mouthfuls of hay;
I sigh at the sight, I feel sick over meals,
　For I'm lone when my shepherd's away.
When dogs eat the grass it is sure to be rain,
　And our dog's in the orchard e'en now;
The swallows fly low, and my heart is in pain,
　While the flies even madden the cow.

The pigeons have moped on the cote the day long,
  And the hens went to roost before noon;
The blackbirds, long still, din the woods with their song,
  And they look upon showers as a boon,
While they keep their nest dry in the wet hazel bush
  And moisten their black sooty wings;
Did they know but my sorrows they'd quickly be hush:
  Birds to make lovers happy should sing.

I've often leaned over the croft's mossy gate
  To listen birds singing at night,
When I for the sure-footed Rover did wait,
  And rich was my bosom's delight.
And sweet had it been now I'm waiting anew
  Till the black snail is out from the grain,
But the south's ruddy clouds they have turned black and blue,
  And the blackbirds are singing for rain.

The thrush 'Wivy wit wivy wit' t'other night
  Sung aloud in the old sallow bush,
And I called him a pert little urchin outright
  To sing 'Heavy wet'; and the thrush
Changed his note in a moment to 'Cheer up' and 'Cheer,'
  And the clouds crept away from the sun,
Till my shepherd he came, and when thrushes I hear
  My heart with the music is won.

But the blackbird is rude and insulting, and now,
  The more the clouds blacken the sky,
The louder he sings from the green hazel bough,
  But he may be sad by and by.
For the cow-boy is stooping beneath the oak tree
  Whose branches hang down to the ground,
And beating his stick on the bushes to see
  If a bird startles out from the sound.

So silence is safety, and, bird, have a care,
  Or your song will your dwelling betray;
For yesterday morning I saw your nest there,
  But sung not to fright you away.

And now the boy's near you; well done, cunning bird,
  You have ceased and popt out t'other side;
Your nest it is safe, not a leaf has he stirred,
  And I have my shepherd descried.

BIRDS' LAMENT

Oh, says the linnet, if I sing,
My love forsook me in the spring,
And nevermore will I be seen
Without my satin gown of green.

Oh, says the pretty-feathered jay,
Now my love is fled away
For the memory of my dear
A feather of each sort I'll wear.

Oh, says the sparrow, my love is gone,
She so much that I doted on,
And e'er since for that selfsame thing
I've made a vow I ne'er will sing.

Oh, says the water-wag-my-tail,
I courted a fair one but could not prevail,
I could not with my love prevail,
So that is the reason I wag my tail.

Oh, says the pretty speckled thrush,
That changes its note from bush to bush,
My love has left me here alone
And I fear she never will return.

Oh, says the rook, and eke the crow,
The reason why in black we go—
Because our love has us forsook,
So pity us, poor crow and rook.

Oh, says the owl, my love has gone,
It was her I doted on;
Since she has gone I know not where to follow,
But after her I'll whoop and hollo.

LANGLEY BUSH

ONE summer's day in happiest mood
  I sat beside old Langley Bush,
And o'er the furze in Hanglands Wood
  I listened at the singing thrush;
Naught did my idle mind engross,
  The tiny flixweed's only flower
Was there, and little beds of moss
  Swelled pleaching to the sunny hour.

I passed it in a sicker day.
  The golden furze-blooms burnt the wind
With sultry sweets—and there I lay
  Tormented with the saddest mind;
The little hill did naked lie,
  The old old bush was broke and gone,
My heart had felt it glad to die
  To miss life's sorrows coming on.

I looked upon its naked stump,
  And pictured back the fallen tree
To days I played hop, skip and jump
  As happy as a boy could be.
I turned me to that happy day
  I streaked beneath its mossy bough,
And there came shadows of dismay,
  So dismally, I feel it now.

I thought o'er all life's sweetest things
  Made dreary as a broken charm,
Wood-ridings where the thrush still sings
  And love went leaning on my arm.
I thought, and felt as desolate
  As want upon a winter scene,
While by that broken stump I sat,
  The type of broken hopes within.

BALLAD

Fair maiden, when my love began,
    Ere thou thy beauty knew,
I fearless owned my passion then
    Nor met reproof from you.

But, now perfection wakes thy charms
    And strangers turn to praise,
Thy pride my faint-grown heart alarms
    And I scarce dare to gaze.

Those lips to which mine own did grow
    In love's glad infancy,
With ruby ripeness now doth glow
    As gems too rich for me.

The full-blown rose thy cheek doth wear,
    Those lilies on thy brow,
Forget whose kiss their buds did bear
    And bloom above me now.

Those eyes, whose first sweet timid light
    Did my young hopes inspire,
Like midday suns in splendour bright
    Now burn me with their fire.

Nor can I weep what I bemoan,
    As great as are my fears;
Too burning is my passion grown
    To e'er be quenched with tears.

HARES AT PLAY

The birds are gone to bed, the cows are still,
And sheep lie panting on each old mole-hill;
And underneath the willow's grey-green bough,
Like toil a-resting, lies the fallow plough.

The timid hares throw daylight fears away
On the lane's road to dust and dance and play,
Then dabble in the grain by naught deterred
To lick the dew-fall from the barley's beard;
Then out they sturt again and round the hill
Like happy thoughts dance, squat, and loiter still,
Till milking maidens in the early morn
Jingle their yokes and sturt them in the corn;
Through well-known beaten paths each nimbling hare
Sturts quick as fear, and seeks its hidden lair.

WINTER MORNING

THE morning wakens with the lumping flails,
Chilly and cold; the early-rising clown
Hurkles along and blows his finger nails;
Icicles from the cottage eaves hang down,
Which peeping children wish for in their play.
The field, once clad in autumn's russet brown,
Spreads from the eye its circle far away
In one huge sheet of snow; from the white wood
The crows all silent seek the dreary fens,
And starnels blacken through the air in crowds;
The sheep stand bleating in their turnip pen
And loathe their frozen food; while labouring men
Button their coats more close from angry clouds
And wish for night and its snug fire agen.

SPRING SONGS

THE blossom-burthened, never-weary May
Again with nature's folks keeps holiday;
Trees hide themselves in green, and happy birds
Sing sweeter songs than can be breathed in words;
The very winds sing sonnets to the sky,
And sunshine bids them welcome—so that I
Feel a new being, as from healthier climes,
And shape my idle fancies into rhymes
Of nature's ecstasy in bursting flowers
And birds nest-building, and sunshiny showers

That on the south-west wind in singing moods
Sprinkle their drops like manna o'er the woods,
Where I still love my careless limbs to fling
Among the shadows of young leafy spring.

SUMMER AMUSEMENTS

I LOVE to hide me on a spot that lies
   In solitudes where footsteps find no track
To make intrusions; there to sympathize
   With nature: often gazing on the rack
That veils the blueness of the summer skies
   In rich varieties; or o'er the grass
Behold the spangled crowds of butterflies
   Flutter from flower to flower, and things that pass
In urgent travel by my still retreat,
   The bustling beetle tribes; and up the stem
Of bents see lady-cows with nimble feet
   Climb tall church-steeple heights—or more to them—
Till at its quaking top they take their seat,
   Which bows, and off they fly fresh happiness to meet.

SUMMER

THE woodman's axe renews its hollow stroke,
   And barkmen's noises in the woods awake,
Ripping the stained bark from the fallen oak,
   Where crumpled fox-fern and the branching brake
Fade 'neath their crushing feet. The timid hare
   Starts from its mossy root or sedgy seat,
And listening foxes leave their startled lair
   And to some blackthorn's spinney make retreat.
Haymakers with their shouldered rakes sojourn
   To hedgy closes, and amid the wheat
The schoolboy runs, while pleasures thickly burn
   Around his heart, to crop corn-bottle flowers,
Scaring the partridge from its quiet bourn,
   That hides for shelter from the summer heat.

THE WOODLAND STILE

WHEN one's been walking in the open plain,
    Where the sun ne'er winks his eye, 'tis sweet awhile
To meet the shadows of a narrow lane
    Or quiet arbour of a woodland stile,
To sit and hear the little bees complain
    Among the woodbine blossoms o'er their toil,
And the hoarse murmurs of the distant swain,
    Driving his horses o'er the sunburnt soil;
While shadows hide me and leaves entertain
    My fancies with their freaks around my seat,
Dancing and whispering with the wooing wind
    Like lovers o'er their secrets; while the heat
Glimmers without and can no passage find
    To hurt the joys which rest so longed to meet.

A HARVEST MORNING

THE mist hangs thick about the early field,
    And many a shout is heard while naught appears
Till close upon the gaze, so thick concealed
    Are things in morning's mist—mayhap her tears
    For summer's sad departure. Silence hears
Brown harvest's ditties that disturb full soon
    Her rest—toil's lusty brawl that daily cheers
Its ignorance of sorrow with the boon
    Of pastoral tunes. Ere morn's red sun appears,
Till dreary evening's ruddy harvest moon
    Hangs its red lamp to light them home again,
The little children in their harvest dress
    Among the stubs of trifling ills complain.

RURAL SCENES

I NEVER saw a man in all my days—
    One whom the calm of quietness pervades—
Who gave not woods and fields his hearty praise
    And felt a happiness in summer shades.

There I meet common thoughts, that all may read
   Who love the quiet fields: I note them well,
Because they give me joy as I proceed,
   And joy renewed when I their beauties tell
In simple verse and unambitious songs,
   That in some mossy cottage haply may
Be read and win the praise of humble tongues
   In the green shadows of some after-day.
For rural fame may likeliest rapture yield
To hearts whose songs are gathered from the field.

WATER-LILIES

THE water-lilies on the meadow stream
   Again spread out their leaves of glossy green;
And some, yet young, of a rich copper gleam,
   Scarce open, in the sunny stream are seen,
Throwing a richness upon leisure's eye,
   That thither wanders in a vacant joy;
While on the sloping banks, luxuriantly,
   Tending of horse and cow, the chubby boy,
In self-delighted whims, will often throw
   Pebbles to hit and splash their sunny leaves;
Yet quickly dry again, they shine and glow
   Like some rich vision that his eye deceives,
Spreading above the water, day by day,
In dangerous deeps, yet out of danger's way.

SUMMER MOODS

I LOVE at eventide to walk alone,
   Down narrow lanes o'erhung with dewy thorn,
Where from the long grass underneath, the snail
   Jet-black creeps out and sprouts his timid horn.
I love to muse o'er meadows newly mown,
   Where withering grass perfumes the sultry air;
Where bees search round with sad and weary drone
   In vain for flowers that bloomed but newly there

While in the juicy corn, the hidden quail
    Cries 'Wet my foot!' and, hid as thoughts unborn,
The fairy-like and seldom seen land-rail
    Utters 'Craik, craik,' like voices underground:
Right glad to meet the evening's dewy veil,
    And see the light fade into glooms around.

EVENING SCHOOLBOYS

HARK to that happy shout!—the school-house door
    Is open thrown, and out the younkers teem;
Some run to leap-frog on the rushy moor,
    And others dabble in the shallow stream,
Catching young fish, and turning pebbles o'er
    For mussel-clams. Look in that mellow gleam,
Where the retiring sun, that rests the while,
    Streams through the broken hedge! How happy seem
Those friendly schoolboys leaning o'er the stile,
    Both reading in one book!—Anon a dream,
Rich with new joys, doth their young hearts beguile,
    And the book's pocketed right hastily.
Ah, happy boys! well may ye turn and smile,
    When joys are yours that never cost a sigh.

THE SHEPHERD'S TREE

HUGE elm, with rifted trunk all notched and scarred,
    Like to a warrior's destiny, I love
To stretch me often on thy shadowed sward,
    And hear the laugh of summer leaves above;
Or on thy buttressed roots to sit, and lean
    In careless attitude, and there reflect
On times and deeds and darings that have been—
    Old castaways, now swallowed in neglect,
While thou art towering in thy strength of heart,
    Stirring the soul to vain imaginings
In which life's sordid being hath no part.
    The wind of that eternal ditty sings
Humming of future things, that burn the mind
To leave some fragment of itself behind.

THE CRAB-TREE

SPRING comes anew and brings each little pledge
   That still, as wont, my childish heart deceives;
I stoop again for violets in the hedge,
   Among the ivy and old withered leaves;
And often mark, amid the clumps of sedge,
   The pooty-shells I gathered when a boy:
But cares have claimed me many an evil day
   And chilled the relish which I had for joy.
Yet when crab-blossoms blush among the may,
   As wont in years gone by, I scramble now
Up mid the bramble for my old esteems,
   Filling my hands with many a blooming bough,
Till the heart-stirring past as present seems,
Save the bright sunshine of those fairy dreams.

THE BREATH OF MORNING

How beautiful and fresh the pastoral smell
   Of tedded hay breathes in this early morn!
Health in these meadows must in summer dwell,
   And take her walks among these fields of corn.
I cannot see her, yet her voice is out
On every breeze that fans my hair about.
   Although the sun is scarcely out of bed,
And leans on ground as half awake from sleep,
   The boy hath left his mossy-thatchèd shed,
And bawls right lustily to cows and sheep;
   Or taken with the woodbines overspread,
Climbs up to pluck them from their thorny bowers,
   Half drowned by dropples pattering on his head
From leaves bemoistened by night's secret showers.

FIRST SIGHT OF SPRING

THE hazel-blooms, in threads of crimson hue,
   Peep through the swelling buds and look for spring
Ere yet a whitethorn leaf appears in view,
   Or March finds throstles pleased enough to sing.

To the old touchwood tree woodpeckers cling
A moment, and their harsh-toned notes renew;
   In happier mood, the stockdove claps his wing;
The squirrel sputters up the powdered oak,
   With tail cocked o'er his head and ears erect,
Startled to hear the woodman's understroke;
   And with the courage which his fears collect,
He hisses fierce half malice and half glee,
Leaping from branch to branch about the tree,
   In winter's foliage, moss and lichens, deckt.

SUMMER EVENING

The frog, haff fearful, jumps across the path,
And little mouse that leaves its hole at eve
Nimbles with timid dread beneath the swath;
My rustling steps awhile their joys deceive,
Till past—and then the cricket sings more strong,
And grasshoppers in merry moods still wear
The short night weary with their fretting song.
Up from behind the mole-hill jumps the hare,
Cheat of his chosen bed, and from the bank
The yellowhammer flutters in short fears
From off its nest hid in the grasses rank,
And drops again when no more noise it hears.
Thus nature's human link and endless thrall,
Proud man, still seems the enemy of all.

THE FEAR OF FLOWERS

The nodding oxeye bends before the wind,
The woodbine quakes lest boys their flowers should find,
And prickly dog-rose, spite of its array,
Can't dare the blossom-seeking hand away,
While thistles wear their heavy knobs of bloom
Proud as a war-horse wears its haughty plume,
And by the roadside danger's self defy;
On commons where pined sheep and oxen lie

In ruddy pomp and ever thronging mood
It stands and spreads like danger in a wood,
And in the village street, where meanest weeds
Can't stand untouched to fill their husks with seeds,
The haughty thistle o'er all danger towers,
In every place the very wasp of flowers.

MARCH

THE insect world, now sunbeams higher climb,
Oft dream of spring, and wake before their time:
Bees stroke their little legs across their wings,
And venture short flights where the snowdrop hings
Its silver bell, and winter aconite
Its buttercup-like flowers that shut at night,
With green leaf furling round its cup of gold,
Like tender maiden muffled from the cold;
They sip and find their honey-dreams are vain,
Then feebly hasten to their hives again.
The butterflies, by eager hopes undone,
Glad as a child come out to greet the sun,
Beneath the shadows of a sunny shower
Are lost, nor see to-morrow's April flower.

AUTUMN

SUMMER is gone and all the merry noise
Of busy harvest in its labouring glee;
The shouts of toil, the laughs of gleaning boys
Sweeing at dinner-hours on willow tree,
The cracking whip, the scraps of homely song,
Sung by the boys that drive the loaded wain,
The noise of geese that haste and hiss along
For corn that litters in the narrow lane
Torn from the wagon by the hedgerow trees,
Tinkles of whetting scythes amid the grain,
The bark of dogs stretched at their panting ease,
Watching the stook where morning's dinner lay—
All these have passed, and silence at her ease
Dreams autumn's melancholy life away.

SCHOOLBOYS IN WINTER

The schoolboys still their morning rambles take
To neighbouring village school with playing speed,
Loitering with pastime's leisure till they quake,
Oft looking up the wild-geese droves to heed,
Watching the letters which their journeys make;
Or plucking haws on which the fieldfares feed,
And hips, and sloes; and on each shallow lake
Making glib slides, where they like shadows go
Till some fresh pastimes in their minds awake.
Then off they start anew and hasty blow
Their numbed and clumpsing fingers till they glow;
Then races with their shadows wildly run
That stride huge giants o'er the shining snow
In the pale splendour of the winter sun.

THE FODDERING BOY

The foddering boy along the crumping snows
With straw-band-belted legs and folded arm
Hastens, and on the blast that keenly blows
Oft turns for breath, and beats his fingers warm,
And shakes the lodging snows from off his clothes,
Buttoning his doublet closer from the storm
And slouching his brown beaver o'er his nose—
Then faces it agen, and seeks the stack
Within its circling fence where hungry lows
Expecting cattle, making many a track
About the snow, impatient for the sound
When in huge forkfuls trailing at his back
He litters the sweet hay about the ground
And brawls to call the staring cattle round.

THE NIGHTINGALE'S NEST

Up this green woodland-ride let's softly rove,
And list the nightingale—she dwells just here.
Hush! let the wood-gate softly clap, for fear
The noise might drive her from her home of love;
For here I've heard her many a merry year—

At morn, at eve, nay, all the livelong day,
As though she lived on song. This very spot,
Just where that old man's beard all wildly trails
Rude arbours o'er the road and stops the way—
And where that child its bluebell flowers hath got,
Laughing and creeping through the mossy rails—
There have I hunted like a very boy,
Creeping on hands and knees through matted thorn
To find her nest and see her feed her young.
And vainly did I many hours employ:
All seemed as hidden as a thought unborn.
And where those crimping fern-leaves ramp among
The hazel's under-boughs, I've nestled down
And watched her while she sung; and her renown
Hath made me marvel that so famed a bird
Should have no better dress than russet brown.
Her wings would tremble in her ecstasy,
And feathers stand on end, as 'twere with joy,
And mouth wide open to release her heart
Of its out-sobbing songs. The happiest part
Of summer's fame she shared, for so to me
Did happy fancies shapen her employ;
But if I touched a bush or scarcely stirred,
All in a moment stopt. I watched in vain:
The timid bird had left the hazel bush,
And at a distance hid to sing again.
Lost in a wilderness of listening leaves,
Rich ecstasy would pour its luscious strain,
Till envy spurred the emulating thrush
To start less wild and scarce inferior songs;
For while of half the year care him bereaves
To damp the ardour of his speckled breast,
The nightingale to summer's life belongs,
And naked trees and winter's nipping wrongs
Are strangers to her music and her rest.
Her joys are evergreen, her world is wide—
Hark! there she is as usual—let's be hush—
For in this blackthorn-clump, if rightly guessed,
Her curious house is hidden. Part aside
These hazel branches in a gentle way

71

And stoop right cautious 'neath the rustling boughs,
For we will have another search to-day
And hunt this fern-strewn thorn-clump round and round
And where this reeded wood-grass idly bows,
We'll wade right through, it is a likely nook:
In such like spots and often on the ground,
They'll build, where rude boys never think to look.
Ay, as I live! her secret nest is here,
Upon this whitethorn stump! I've searched about
For hours in vain. There ! put that bramble by—
Nay, trample on its branches and get near.
How subtle is the bird! she started out,
And raised a plaintive note of danger nigh,
Ere we were past the brambles; and now, near
Her nest, she sudden stops—as choking fear
That might betray her home. So even now
We'll leave it as we found it: safety's guard
Of pathless solitudes shall keep it still.
See there! she's sitting on the old oak bough,
Mute in her fears; our presence doth retard
Her joys, and doubt turns every rapture chill.
Sing on, sweet bird! may no worse hap befall
Thy visions than the fear that now deceives.
We will not plunder music of its dower,
Nor turn this spot of happiness to thrall;
For melody seems hid in every flower
That blossoms near thy home. These harebells all
Seem bowing with the beautiful in song;
And gaping orchis, with its spotted leaves,
Seems blushing with the singing it has heard.
How curious is the nest! no other bird
Uses such loose materials, or weaves
Its dwelling in such spots: dead oaken leaves
Are placed without and velvet moss within,
And little scraps of grass, and—scant and spare,
Of what seem scarce materials—down and hair;
For from men's haunts she nothing seems to win.
Yet nature is the builder, and contrives
Homes for her children's comfort even here,
Where solitude's disciples spend their lives

Unseen, save when a wanderer passes near
Who loves such pleasant places.   Deep adown
The nest is made, a hermit's mossy cell.
Snug lie her curious eggs in number five,
Of deadened green, or rather olive-brown;
And the old prickly thorn-bush guards them well.
So here we'll leave them, still unknown to wrong,
As the old woodland's legacy of song.

THE SKYLARK

THE rolls and harrows lie at rest beside
The battered road; and spreading far and wide
Above the russet clods, the corn is seen
Sprouting its spiry points of tender green,
Where squats the hare, to terrors wide awake,
Like some brown clod the harrows failed to break.
Opening their golden caskets to the sun,
The buttercups make schoolboys eager run,
To see who shall be first to pluck the prize—
Up from their hurry, see, the skylark flies,
And o'er her half-formed nest, with happy wings
Winnows the air, till in the cloud she sings,
Then hangs a dust-spot in the sunny skies,
And drops, and drops, till in her nest she lies,
Which they unheeded passed—not dreaming then
That birds which flew so high would drop agen
To nests upon the ground, which anything
May come at to destroy.   Had they the wing
Like such a bird, themselves would be too proud,
And build on nothing but a passing cloud!
As free from danger as the heavens are free
From pain and toil, there would they build and be,
And sail about the world to scenes unheard
Of and unseen—Oh, were they but a bird!
So think they, while they listen to its song,
And smile and fancy and so pass along;
While its low nest, moist with the dews of morn,
Lies safely, with the leveret, in the corn.

DOVES

ROAMING the little path 'neath dotterel trees
Of some old hedge or spinney side, I've oft
Been startled pleasantly from musing ways
By frighted doves that suddenly aloft
Spring through the many boughs with chittering noise;
Till, free from such restraints, above the head
They smacked their clapping wings for very joys;
And in a curious mood I've oft been led
To climb the twig-surrounded trunk, and there
On some few bits of sticks two white eggs lie,
As left by accident all lorn and bare,
Almost without a nest; yet by and by
Two birds in golden down will leave the shells
And hiss and snap at wind-blown leaves that shake
Around their home where green seclusion dwells;
Till fledged, and then the young adventurers take
The old ones timid flights from oak to oak,
Listening the pleasant sutherings of the shade,
Nor startled by the woodman's hollow stroke;
Till autumn's pleasant visions pine and fade,
Then they in bolder crowds will sweep and fly
And brave the desert of a winter sky.

THE YELLOW WAGTAIL'S NEST

UPON an eddying in a quiet nook
(We double down choice places in a book,
And this I noted as a pleasant scene,
Hemmed in all round with barley's juicy green),
In the thick clover-grass, at holiday,
A broken plough as leisure's partner lay,
A pleasant bench among the grass and flowers
For merry weeders in their dinner hours,
From fallow fields released and hot turmoil;
It nestled like a thought, forgot by toil,
And seemed so picturesque a place for rest
I e'en dropped down to be a minute's guest;
And as I bent me for a flower to stoop,
A little bird cheeped loud and fluttered up;

74

The grasses tottered with their husky seeds,
That ramped beside the plough with ranker weeds;
I looked—and there a snug nest deep and dry
Of roots and twitches entertained my eye,
And six eggs sprinkled o'er with spots of grey
Lay snug as comfort's wishes ever lay.
The yellow wagtail fixed its dwelling there,
Sheltered from rainfalls by the shelving share,
That leaned above it like a sheltering roof
From rain and wind and tempest comfort-proof.
Such safety-places little birds will find
Far from the cares and help of humankind;
For nature is their kind protector still
To choose their dwellings furthest off from ill;
So thought I, sitting on that broken plough,
While evening's sunshine gleamed upon my brow,
So soft, so sweet; and I so happy then
Felt life still Eden from the haunts of men.

THE PEWIT'S NEST

ACROSS the fallow clods at early morn
I took a random track where, scant and spare,
The grass and nibbled leaves, all closely shorn,
Leave a burnt flat all bleaching brown and bare,
Where hungry sheep in freedom range forlorn;
And 'neath the leaning willow and odd thorn
And mole-hill large that vagrant shade supplies,
They batter round to shun the teasing flies,
Trampling smooth places hard as cottage floors,
Where the time-killing lonely shepherd boys,
Whose summer homes are ever out of doors,
Their chock-holes form and chalk their marble ring
And make their clay taws at the bubbling spring;
And in their wrangling sport and gambling joys
They strime their clock-like shadows—when it cloys
To guess the hour that slowly runs away—
And shorten sultry turmoil with their play.
Here did I roam while veering overhead
The pewit whirred in many whewing rings
And 'chewsit' screamed and clapped her flapping wings.

To hunt her nest my rambling step was led
O'er the broad baulk beset with little hills
By moles long formed and pismires tenanted
As likely spots—but still I searched in vain:
When all at once the noisy birds were still,
And on the lands a furrowed ridge between,
Chance found four eggs of dingy dirty green,
Deep blotched with plashy spots of chocolate stain;
Their small ends inward turned as ever found,
As though some curious hand had laid them round,
Yet lying on the ground with naught at all
Of soft grass, withered twitch and bleachèd weed
To keep them from the rain-storms' frequent fall;
And here she broods on her unsavoury bed.
When by and by, with little care and heed,
Her young, with each a shell upon its head,
Run after their wild parent's restless cry,
And from their own fear's tiny shadows run
'Neath clods and stones to cringe and snugly lie,
Hid from all sight but the all-seeing sun
Till never-ceasing danger seemeth by.

THE LARK'S NEST

FROM yon black clump of wheat that grows
　　More rank and higher than the rest,
A lark—I marked her as she rose—
　　At early morning left her nest.
Her eggs were four of dusky hue,
　　Blotched brown as is the very ground,
With tinges of a purply hue
　　The larger ends encircling round.

Behind a clod how snug the nest
　　Is in a horse's footing fixed!
Of twitch and stubbles roughly dressed,
　　With roots and horsehair intermixed.
The wheat surrounds it like a bower,
　　And like to thatch each bowing blade
Throws off the frequent falling shower
　　　　—And here's an egg this morning laid!

76

THE SWALLOW'S NEST

HERE down the meadow runs a path
  Snake-winding through the pleasant hay,
That leadeth over many a swath
  Which shed their fragrance all the way.
At last the eye beholds the view
  Of many arches all a-row,
That leads the traveller safely through
  When floods are roaring loud below.

There 'neath an arch, as like to drop,
  Two hermit swallows yearly fix
Their nest beneath the freestone top—
  You'd almost wonder how it sticks.
And through and through the brig they whip—
  Thoughts hardly can the pace maintain—
Then 'twit' and in the water dip,
  And 'twit' and hurry back again.

THE MOOR-HEN'S NEST

I IN my summer rambles love to see
A flood-washed bank support an aged tree,
Whose roots are bare; yet some with foothold good
Crankle and spread and strike beneath the flood;
Yet still it leans as safer hold to win
On t'other side, and seems as tumbling in.
Yet every summer finds it green and gay
And winter leaves it safe as did the May;
Nor does the moor-hen find its safety vain,
For on its roots their last year's homes remain;
And once again a couple from the brood
Seek their old birthplace, and in safety's mood
Build up their flags and lay; though danger comes,
It dares and tries and cannot reach their homes;
And still they hatch their eggs and sweetly dream
On their shelfed nest hung just to touch the stream;
And soon their sooty brood from fear elope
Where bulrush forests give them sweeter hope;

Their hanging nest that aids their wishes well
Each leaves for water as it leaves the shell;
They dive and dare and every gambol try
Till they themselves to other scenes can fly.

REMEMBRANCES

SUMMER'S pleasures they are gone like to visions every one,
And the cloudy days of autumn and of winter cometh on.
I tried to call them back, but unbidden they are gone
Far away from heart and eye and for ever far away
Dear heart, and can it be that such raptures meet decay?
I thought them all eternal when by Langley Bush I lay,
I thought them joys eternal when I used to shout and play
On its bank at 'clink and bandy,' 'chock' and 'taw' and 'duck-
    ing-stone,'
Where silence sitteth now on the wild heath as her own
Like a ruin of the past all alone.

When I used to lie and sing by old Eastwell's boiling spring,
When I used to tie the willow boughs together for a swing,
And fish with crooked pins and thread and never catch a thing,
With heart just like a feather, now as heavy as a stone;
When beneath old Lea Close Oak I the bottom branches broke
To make our harvest cart like so many working folk,
And then to cut a straw at the brook to have a soak.
Oh, I never dreamed of parting or that trouble had a sting,
Or that pleasures like a flock of birds would ever take to wing,
Leaving nothing but a little naked spring.

When jumping time away on old Crossberry Way,
And eating haws like sugarplums ere they had lost the may,
And skipping like a leveret before the peep of day
On the roly-poly up and downs of pleasant Swordy Well,
When in Round Oak's narrow lane as the south got black again
We sought the hollow ash that was shelter from the rain,
With our pockets full of peas we had stolen from the grain;
How delicious was the dinner-time on such a showery day!
Oh, words are poor receipts for what time hath stole away,
The ancient pulpit trees and the play.

When for school o'er Little Field with its brook and wooden
    brig,
Where I swaggered like a man though I was not half so big,
While I held my little plough though 'twas but a willow
    twig,
And drove my team along made of nothing but a name,
'Gee hep' and 'hoit' and 'woi'—oh, I never call to mind
These pleasant names of places but I leave a sigh behind,
While I see the little mouldiwarps hang sweeing to the wind
On the only aged willow that in all the field remains,
And nature hides her face while they're sweeing in their
    chains
And in a silent murmuring complains.

Here was commons for their hills, where they seek for freedom
    still,
Though every common's gone and though traps are set to kill
The little homeless miners—oh, it turns my bosom chill
When I think of old Sneap Green, Puddock's Nook and Hilly
    Snow,
Where bramble bushes grew and the daisy gemmed in dew
And the hills of silken grass like to cushions to the view,
Where we threw the pismire crumbs when we'd nothing else
    to do,
All levelled like a desert by the never-weary plough,
All vanished like the sun where that cloud is passing now
And settled here for ever on its brow.

Oh, I never thought that joys would run away from boys,
Or that boys would change their minds and forsake such
    summer joys;
But alack, I never dreamed that the world had other toys
To petrify first feeling like the fable into stone,
Till I found the pleasure past and a winter come at last,
Then the fields were sudden bare and the sky got overcast,
And boyhood's pleasing haunts, like a blossom in the blast,
Was shrivelled to a withered weed and trampled down and
    done,
Till vanished was the morning spring and set the summer sun,
And winter fought her battle strife and won.

By Langley Bush I roam, but the bush hath left its hill,
On Cowper Green I stray, 'tis a desert strange and chill,
And the spreading Lea Close Oak, ere decay had penned its
    will,
To the axe of the spoiler and self-interest fell a prey,
And Crossberry Way and old Round Oak's narrow lane
With its hollow trees like pulpits I shall never see again,
Enclosure like a Buonaparte let not a thing remain,
It levelled every bush and tree and levelled every hill
And hung the moles for traitors—though the brook is running
    still
It runs a naked stream, cold and chill.

Oh, had I known as then joy had left the paths of men,
I had watched her night and day, be sure, and never slept agen,
And when she turned to go, oh, I'd caught her mantle then,
And wooed her like a lover by my lonely side to stay;
Ay, knelt and worshipped on, as love in beauty's bower,
And clung upon her smiles as a bee upon a flower,
And gave her heart my posies, all cropt in a sunny hour,
As keepsakes and pledges all to never fade away;
But love never heeded to treasure up the may,
So it went the common road to decay.

SONG'S ETERNITY

WHAT is song's eternity?
   Come and see.
Can it noise and bustle be?
   Come and see.
Praises sung or praises said
   Can it be?
Wait awhile and these are dead—
   Sigh, sigh;
Be they high or lowly bred
   They die.

What is song's eternity?
   Come and see.
Melodies of earth and sky,
   Here they be.

Song once sung to Adam's ears
  Can it be?
Ballads of six thousand years
  Thrive, thrive;
Songs awakened with the spheres
  Alive.

Mighty songs that miss decay,
  What are they?
Crowds and cities pass away
  Like a day.
Books are writ and books are read;
  What are they?
Years will lay them with the dead—
  Sigh, sigh;
Trifles unto nothing wed,
  They die.

Dreamers, list the honey-bee;
  Mark the tree
Where the bluecap, 'tootle tee,'
  Sings a glee
Sung to Adam and to Eve—
  Here they be.
When floods covered every bough,
  Noah's ark
Heard that ballad singing now;
  Hark, hark,

'Tootle tootle tootle tee'—
  Can it be
Pride and fame must shadows be?
  Come and see—
Every season owns her own;
  Bird and bee
Sing creation's music on;
  Nature's glee
Is in every mood and tone
  Eternity.

The eternity of song
  Liveth here;
Nature's universal tongue
  Singeth here
Songs I've heard and felt and seen
  Everywhere;
Songs like the grass are evergreen:
  The giver
Said 'Live and be'—and they have been,
  For ever.[1]

COUNTRY LETTER

DEAR brother Robin, this comes from us all
With our kind love, and could Gip write and all
Though but a dog he'd have his love to spare,
For still he knows, and by your corner chair
The moment he comes in he lies him down
And seems to fancy you are in the town.
This leaves us well in health, thank God for that!
For old acquaintance Sue has kept your hat
Which mother brushes ere she lays it by
And every Sunday goes upstairs to cry.
Jane still is yours till you come back agen
And ne'er so much as dances with the men;
And Ned the woodman every week comes in
And asks about you kindly as our kin;
And he with this and goody Thompson sends
Remembrances with those of all our friends.
Father with us sends love until he hears
And mother she has nothing but her tears,
Yet wishes you like us in health the same
And longs to see a letter with your name,
So, loving brother, don't forget to write.
Old Gip lies on the hearth stone every night;
Mother can't bear to turn him out of doors
And never noises now of dirty floors;
Father will laugh but lets her have her way,
And Gip for kindness get a double pay.

[1] The last stanza appears by itself in another MS

So Robin write and let us quickly see
You don't forget old friends no more than we,
Nor let my mother have so much to blame
To go three journeys ere your letter came.

THE FENS

WANDERING by the river's edge,
I love to rustle through the sedge
And through the woods of reed to tear
Almost as high as bushes are.
Yet, turning quick with shudder chill,
As danger ever does from ill,
Fear's moment-ague quakes the blood,
While plop the snake coils in the flood

And, hissing with a forkèd tongue,
Across the river winds along.
In coat of orange, green, and blue
Now on a willow branch I view,
Grey waving to the sunny gleam,
Kingfishers watch the ripple stream
For little fish that nimble by
And in the gravel shallows lie.

Eddies run before the boats,
Gurgling where the fisher floats,
Who takes advantage of the gale
And hoists his handkerchief for sail
On osier twigs that form a mast—
And quick his nutshell hurries past,
While idly lies, nor wanted more,
The sprit that pushed him on before.

There's not a hill in all the view,
Save that a forkèd cloud or two
Upon the verge of distance lies
And into mountains cheats the eyes.
And as to trees, the willows wear
Lopped heads as high as bushes are;

Some taller things the distance shrouds,
That may be trees or stacks or clouds,
Or may be nothing; still they wear
A semblance where there's naught to spare.

Among the tawny tasselled reed
The ducks and ducklings float and feed.
With head oft dabbing in the flood
They fish all day the weedy mud,
And tumbler-like are bobbing there,
Heels topsy-turvy in the air,
Then up and quack and down they go,
Heels over head again below.

The geese in troops come droving up,
Nibble the weeds, and take a sup;
And closely puzzled to agree,
Chatter like gossips over tea.
The gander with his scarlet nose
When strife's at height will interpose;
And, stretching neck to that and this,
With now a mutter, now a hiss,
A nibble at the feathers too,
A sort of 'Pray be quiet, do,'
And turning as the matter mends,
He stills them into mutual friends;
Then in a sort of triumph sings
And throws the water o'er his wings.

Ah, could I see a spinney nigh,
A puddock riding in the sky
Above the oaks with easy sail
On stilly wings and forkèd tail,
Or meet a heath of furze in flower,
I might enjoy a quiet hour,
Sit down at rest, and walk at ease,
And find a many things to please.
But here my fancy's moods admire
The naked levels till they tire,
Nor e'en a mole-hill cushion meet
To rest on when I want a seat.

Here's little save the river scene,
And grounds of oats in rustling green,
And crowded growth of wheat and beans,
That with the hope of plenty leans
And cheers the farmer's gazing brow,
Who lives and triumphs in the plough.
One sometimes meets a pleasant sward
Of swarthy grass; and quickly marred,
The plough soon turns it into brown,
And, when again one rambles down
The path, small hillocks meet the eye
And smoke beneath a burning sky.
Green paddocks have but little charms
With gain the merchandise of farms;
And, muse and marvel where we may,
Gain mars the landscape every day—

The meadow grass turned up and copt,
The trees to stumpy dotterels lopt,
The hearth with fuel to supply
For rest to smoke and chatter by;
Giving the joy of home delights,
The warmest mirth on coldest nights.
And so for gain, that joys repay,
Change cheats the landscapes every day,
Nor trees nor bush about it grows
That from the hatchet can repose,
And the horizon stooping smiles
O'er treeless fens of many miles.
Spring comes and goes and comes agen,
And all is nakedness and fen.

SPEAR-THISTLE

WHERE the broad sheepwalk opens bare and brown
  With scant grass ever pining after showers,
And unchecked winds go fanning up and down
  The little strawy bents and nodding flowers,
There the huge thistle, spurred with many thorns,
The sun-crackt upland's russet swells adorns,

Not undevoid of beauty there they come,
    Armed warriors, waiting neither suns nor showers,
Guarding the little clover plots to bloom
    While sheep nor oxen dare not crop their flowers
Unsheathing their own knobs of tawny flowers
When summer cometh in her hottest hours.

The pewit, swopping up and down
    And screaming round the passer-by,
Or running o'er the herbage brown
    With copple crown uplifted high,
Loves in its clumps to make a home
Where danger seldom cares to come.

The yellow-hammer, often prest
    For spot to build and be unseen,
Will in its shelter trust her nest
    When fields and meadows glow with green;
And larks, though paths go closely by,
Will in its shade securely lie.

The partridge, too, that scarce can trust
    The open downs to be at rest,
Will in its clumps lie down, and dust
    And prune its horseshoe-circled breast,
And oft in shining fields of green
Will lay and raise its brood unseen.

The sheep, when hunger presses sore,
    May nip the clover round its nest;
But soon the thistle, wounding sore,
    Relieves it from each brushing guest,
That leaves a bit of wool behind,
The yellow-hammer loves to find.

The horse will set his foot and bite
    Close to the ground-lark's guarded nest
And snort to meet the prickly sight;
    He fans the feathers of her breast—
Yet thistles prick so deep that he
Turns back and leaves her dwelling free.

86

Its prickly knobs the dews of morn
    Doth bead with dressing rich to see,
When threads doth hang from thorn to thorn
    Like the small spinner's tapestry;
And from the flowers a sultry smell
Comes that agrees with summer well.

The bee will make its bloom a bed,
    The bumble-bee in tawny brown;
And one in jacket fringed with red
    Will rest upon its velvet down
When overtaken in the rain,
And wait till sunshine comes again.

And there are times when travel goes
    Along the sheep-tracks' beaten ways,
Then pleasure many a praise bestows
    Upon its blossoms' pointed rays,
When other things are parched beside
And hot day leaves it in its pride.

WINTER IN THE FENS

So moping flat and low our valleys lie,
So dull and muggy is our winter sky,
Drizzling from day to day with threats of rain,
And when that falls still threatening on again;
From one wet week so great an ocean flows
That every village to an island grows,
And every road for even weeks to come
Is stopt, and none but horsemen go from home;
And one wet night leaves travel's best in doubt
And horseback travellers ask if floods are out
Of every passer-by, and with their horse
The meadow's ocean try in vain to cross;
The horse's footings with a sucking sound
Fill up with water on the firmest ground,

And ruts that dribble into brooks elsewhere
Can find no fall or flat to dribble here;
But filled with wet they brim and overflow
Till hollows in the road to rivers grow;
Then wind with sudden rage, abrupt and blea,
Twirls every lingering leaf from off each tree.
Such is our lowland scene that winter gives,
And strangers wonder where our comfort lives;
Yet in a little close, however keen
The winter comes, I find a patch of green,
Where robins, by the miser winter made
Domestic, flirt and perch upon the spade;
And in a little garden-close at home
I watch for spring—and there's the crocus come!

MORNING SHOWERS

Now the meadow water smokes,
And the hedgerow's dripping oaks
Pitter-patter all around
And dimple the once dusty ground;
The spinners' threads about the weeds
Are hung with little drops in beads;
Clover silver-green becomes,
And purple-blue surrounds the plums,
And every place breathes fresh and fair
When morning pays her visit there.

The waterfowl with suthering wing
Dive down the river, splash and spring
Up to the very clouds again
That sprinkle scuds of coming rain,
That fly and drizzle all the day
Till dripping grass is turned to grey;
The various clouds [now] move or lie
Like mighty travellers in the sky,
All mountainous and ridged and curled,
That may have travelled round the world.

When the rain at midday stops,
Spandles glitter in the drops,
And, as each thread a sunbeam was,
Cobwebs glitter in the grass.
The sheep all loaded with the rain
Try to shake it off again,
And ere dried by wind and sun
The load will scarcely let them run.

THE MEADOW LAKE

I'VE often gazed with pleasure by the edge
Of the old meadow lake, floodwashed and crook'd,
The water-rat slow rustling in the sedge,
The fish-ring wavering in the clear; I've looked
In rapture on the mellow summer shine
Of the still water gleaming in the sun,
Just wrinkled by the plash of quiet kine
Who knee-deep in the flags would drink—and done,
Back to their feed on the shorn sward again;
The flags, the bulrush, and the barbed leaf
Of water-weed, bethread with lighter vein,
And water-lily giving flies relief,
Who float half drowsy to its sheltering bay—
These lie close on the water and still dry:
If dropples plash upon them from the spring
Of playful fish, they scarce a moment lie
But roll like water from the moor-hen's wing,
Its oily green still sunny as before.
Thus musing on the brink, a startled fright
Comes with a sudden plunge from t'other side,
And flags and rush in quick disorder start
When instant, musing shepherd is descried,
Whose dog ran forward with a gladsome heart
To hunt the water-rat and scared moor-hen
Who dives and flounders and then dives agen;
Till weary quite, once more he seeks the side,
And shakes the water from his dripping hide,
And rolls upon the grass and dances round
The shepherd as he soodles round the ground.

LABOUR'S LEISURE

OH, for the feelings and the careless health
That found me toiling in the fields, the joy
I felt at eve with not a wish for wealth,
When, labour done and in the hedge put by
My delving spade, I homeward used to hie
With thoughts of books I often read by stealth
Beneath the blackthorn clumps at dinner-hour;
It urged my weary feet with eager speed
To hasten home where winter fire did shower
Scant light, now felt as beautiful indeed
Where bending o'er my knees I used to read
With earnest heed all books that had the power
To give me joy in most delicious ways
And rest my spirits after weary days.

YOUNG LAMBS

THE spring is coming by a many signs;
    The trays are up, the hedges broken down,
That fenced the haystack, and the remnant shines
    Like some old antique fragment weathered brown.
And where suns peep, in every sheltered place,
    The little early buttercups unfold
A glittering star or two—till many trace
    The edges of the blackthorn clumps in gold.
And then a little lamb bolts up behind
    The hill and wags his tail to meet the yoe,
And then another, sheltered from the wind,
    Lies all his length as dead—and lets me go
Close by and never stirs, but beaking lies,
    With legs stretched out as though he could not rise.

SIGNS OF WINTER

THE cat runs races with her tail. The dog
Leaps o'er the orchard hedge and knarls the grass.
The swine run round and grunt and play with straw,
Snatching out hasty mouthfuls from the stack.

Sudden upon the elm-tree tops the crow
Unceremonious visit pays and croaks,
Then swops away. From mossy barn the owl
Bobs hasty out—wheels round and, scared as soon,
As hastily retires. The ducks grow wild
And from the muddy pond fly up and wheel
A circle round the village and soon, tired,
Plunge in the pond again. The maids in haste
Snatch from the orchard hedge the mizzled clothes
And laughing hurry in to keep them dry.

WINTER EVENING

THE crib stock fothered, horses suppered up,
And cows in sheds all littered down in straw,
The threshers gone, the owls are left to whoop,
The ducks go waddling with distended craw
Through little hole made in the hen-roost door,
And geese with idle gabble never o'er
Bait careless hog until he tumbles down,
Insult provoking spite to noise the more;
While fowl high-perched blink with contemptuous
     frown
On all the noise and bother heard below ;
Over the stable-ridge in crowds, the crow,
With jackdaws intermixed, known by their noise,
To the warm woods behind the village go;
And whistling home for bed go weary boys.

APRIL SHOWERS

DELIGHTFUL weather for all sorts of moods!
And most for him grey morn and swarthy eve
Found rambling up the little narrow lane
Where primrose banks amid the hazelly woods
Peep most delightfully on passers-by;
While April's little clouds about the sky
Mottle and freak and unto fancy lie

91

Idling and ending travel for the day;
Till darker clouds sail up with cumbrous heave
South o'er the woods and scare them all away;
Then comes the rain, pelting with pearly drops
The primrose crowds until they stoop and lie
All fragrance to his mind that musing stops
Beneath the hawthorn till the shower is by.

FIR-WOOD

THE fir-trees taper into twigs and wear
The rich blue-green of summer all the year,
Softening the roughest tempest almost calm
And offering shelter ever still and warm
To the small path that travels underneath,
Where loudest winds—almost as summer's breath—
Scarce fan the weed that lingers green below
When others out of doors are lost in snow.
And sweet the music trembles on the ear
As the wind suthers through each tiny spear,
Makeshifts for leaves; and yet, so rich they show,
Winter is almost summer where they grow.

GRASSHOPPERS

GRASSHOPPERS go in many a thrumming spring
And now to stalks of tasselled sour-grass cling,
That shakes and swees awhile, but still keeps straight;
While arching oxeye doubles with his weight.
Next on the cat-tail grass with farther bound
He springs, that bends until they touch the ground.

BADGER

WHEN midnight comes a host of dogs and men
Go out and track the badger to his den,
And put a sack within the hole, and lie
Till the old grunting badger passes by.

He comes and hears—they let the strongest loose.
The old fox hears the noise and drops the goose.
The poacher shoots and hurries from the cry,
And the old hare half wounded buzzes by.
They get a forkèd stick to bear him down
And clap the dogs and take him to the town,
And bait him all the day with many dogs,
And laugh and shout and fright the scampering hogs.
He runs along and bites at all he meets:
They shout and hollo down the noisy streets.

He turns about to face the loud uproar
And drives the rebels to their very door.
The frequent stone is hurled where'er they go;
When badgers fight, then every one's a foe.
The dogs are clapt and urged to join the fray;
The badger turns and drives them all away.
Though scarcely half as big, demure and small,
He fights with dogs for hours and beats them all.
The heavy mastiff, savage in the fray,
Lies down and licks his feet and turns away.
The bulldog knows his match and waxes cold,
The badger grins and never leaves his hold.
He drives the crowd and follows at their heels
And bites them through—the drunkard swears and reels

The frighted women take the boys away,
The blackguard laughs and hurries on the fray.
He tries to reach the woods, an awkward race,
But sticks and cudgels quickly stop the chase.
He turns agen and drives the noisy crowd
And beats the many dogs in noises loud.
He drives away and beats them every one,
And then they loose them all and set them on.
He falls as dead and kicked by boys and men,
Then starts and grins and drives the crowd agen;
Till kicked and torn and beaten out he lies
And leaves his hold and cackles, groans, and dies.

THE FOX

THE shepherd on his journey heard when nigh
His dog among the bushes barking high;
The ploughman ran and gave a hearty shout,
He found a weary fox and beat him out.
The ploughman laughed and would have ploughed him in,
But the old shepherd took him for the skin.
He lay upon the furrow stretched for dead,
The old dog lay and licked the wounds that bled,
The ploughman beat him till his ribs would crack,
And then the shepherd slung him at his back;
And when he rested, to his dog's surprise,
The old fox started from his dead disguise;
And while the dog lay panting in the sedge
He up and snapt and bolted through the hedge.

He scampered to the bushes far away;
The shepherd called the ploughman to the fray;
The ploughman wished he had a gun to shoot.
The old dog barked and followed the pursuit.
The shepherd threw his hook and tottered past;
The ploughman ran, but none could go so fast;
The woodman threw his faggot from the way
And ceased to chop and wondered at the fray.
But when he saw the dog and heard the cry
He threw his hatchet—but the fox was by.
The shepherd broke his hook and lost the skin;
He found a badger-hole and bolted in.
They tried to dig, but, safe from danger's way,
He lived to chase the hounds another day.

THE VIXEN

AMONG the taller wood with ivy hung,
The old fox plays and dances round her young.
She snuffs and barks if any passes by
And swings her tail and turns prepared to fly.
The horseman hurries by, she bolts to see,
And turns agen, from danger never free.

If any stands she runs among the poles
And barks and snaps and drives them in the holes.
The shepherd sees them and the boy goes by
And gets a stick and progs the hole to try.
They get all still and lie in safety sure,
And out again when everything's secure,
And start and snap at blackbirds bouncing by
To fight and catch the great white butterfly.

QUAIL'S NEST

I WANDERED out one rainy day
    And heard a bird with merry joys
Cry 'wet my foot' for half the way;
    I stood and wondered at the noise,

When from my foot a bird did flee—
    The rain flew bouncing from her breast—
I wondered what the bird could be,
    And almost trampled on her nest.

The nest was full of eggs and round;
    I met a shepherd in the vales,
And stood to tell him what I found.
    He knew and said it was a quail's,

For he himself the nest had found,
    Among the wheat and on the green,
When going on his daily round,
    With eggs as many as fifteen.

Among the stranger birds they feed,
    Their summer flight is short and low;
There's very few know where they breed,
    And scarcely any where they go.

BLACKBIRD'S NEST

THE cloudy morning brought a pleasant day,
And soon the busy mist was all away,
When first I wandered out and chanced to see
A woodbine twining round a stoven tree,

That ventured up and formed a bush at top
And bended leaning till it met a prop,
And overhung with leaves so thick a shade
You couldn't see the nest the blackbird made,
Who fluttered o'er my head as if from boys;
And soon her partner answered to the noise.
The path went closely by, but seldom prest
By passer-by, who never saw the nest;
The old birds sat and sung in safety sure,
And the young brood, pin-feathered, lay secure.

FARMER'S BOY

He waits all day beside his little flock
And asks the passing stranger what's o'clock,
But those who often pass his daily tasks
Look at their watch and tell before he asks.
He mutters stories to himself and lies
Where the thick hedge the warmest house supplies,
And when he hears the hunters far and wide
He climbs the highest tree to see them ride—
He climbs till all the fields are blea and bare
And makes the old crow's nest an easy-chair.
And soon his sheep are got in other grounds—
He hastens down and fears his master come,
He stops the gap and keeps them all in bounds
And tends them closely till it's time for home.

MARKET DAY

With arms and legs at work and gentle stroke
That urges switching tail nor mends his pace,
On an old ribbed and weather-beaten horse,
The farmer goes jogtrotting to the fair,
Both keep their pace that nothing can provoke,
Followed by brindled dog that snuffs the ground
With urging bark and hurries at his heels.
His hat slouched down, and greatcoat buttoned close

Bellied like hoopèd keg, and chuffy face
Red as the morning sun, he takes his round
And talks of stock: and when his jobs are done
And Dobbin's hay is eaten from the rack,
He drinks success to corn in language hoarse,
And claps old Dobbin's hide, and potters back.

THE LOUT (I)

No sort of learning ever hurts his head;
He buys a song and never hears it read;
He gets the tune and never heeds the words;
His pocket, too, a penny oft affords
To buy a book, no matter what about,
And there he keeps it till he wears it out.
In every job he's sure to have a share,
And shouts to haste his speed he cannot bear.
He seldom seeks the house in leisure hour,
But finds the haystack in a sudden shower,
And hid from all he there contrives to lie,
Rain how it will, to keep his garments dry.
He owns one suit and wears it all the week,
A dirty slop as dingy as his cheek.

THE LOUT (II)

For Sunday's play he never makes excuse,
But plays at taw, and buys his Spanish juice.
Hard as his toil, and ever slow to speak,
Yet he gives maidens many a burning cheek;
For none can pass him but his witless grace
Of bawdry brings the blushes in her face.
As vulgar as the dirt he treads upon,
He calls his cows or drives his horses on;
He knows the tamest cow and strokes her side
And often tries to mount her back and ride,
And takes her tail at night in idle play,
And makes her drag him homeward all the way.
He knows of nothing but the football match,
And where hens lay, and when the duck will hatch,

97

THE LOUT (III)

HE plays with other boys when work is done,
But feels too clumsy and too stiff to run,
Yet where there's mischief he can find a way
The first to join and last [to run] away.
What's said or done he never heeds or minds
But gets his pence for all the eggs he finds.
He thinks his master's horses far the best,
And always labours longer than the rest.
In frost and cold though lame he's forced to go—
The call's more urgent when he journeys slow.
In surly speed he helps the maids by force
And feeds the cows and hallos till he's hoarse;
And when he's lame they only jest and play
And bid him throw his kiby heels away.

STONE-PIT

THE passing traveller with wonder sees
A deep and ancient stone-pit full of trees;
So deep and very deep the place has been,
The church might stand within and not be seen.
The passing stranger oft with wonder stops
And thinks he e'en could walk upon their tops,
And often stoops to see the busy crow,
And stands above and sees the eggs below;
And while the wild horse gives its head a toss,
The squirrel dances up and runs across.
The boy that stands and kills the black-nosed bee
Dares down as soon as magpies' nest are found,
And wonders when he climbs the highest tree
To find it reaches scarce above the ground.

FARM BREAKFAST

MAIDS shout to breakfast in a merry strife,
And the cat runs to hear the whetted knife,
And dogs are ever in the way to watch
The mouldy crust and falling bone to catch.

The wooden dishes round in haste are set,
And round the table all the boys are met;
All know their own save Hodge who would be first,
But every one his master leaves the worst.
On every wooden dish, a humble claim,
Two rude-cut letters mark the owner's name;
From every nook the smile of plenty calls,
And reasty flitches decorate the walls,
Moore's Almanack where wonders never cease—
All smeared with candle-snuff and bacon-grease.

A HILL-SIDE HOUSE

THERE is a house stands in a lonely way,
The hill seems falling on it all the day;
It seems half-hidden, like a robber's den,
And seems more safe for robbers than for men.
The trees look bushes scarcely half as big,
Seem taking root and growing on the rig.
The cows that travel up with little heed
Seem looking down upon the roof to feed,
And if they take a step or stumble more
They seem in danger then of tumbling o'er.
The cocks and hens that fill a little space
Are all that look like home about the place.
The woods seem ready on the house to drop,
And rabbits breed above the chimney-top.

NOVEMBER

THE shepherds almost wonder where they dwell,
And the old dog for his right journey stares:
The path leads somewhere, but they cannot tell,
And neighbour meets with neighbour unawares.
The maiden passes close beside her cow,
And wanders on, and thinks her far away;
The ploughman goes unseen behind his plough
And seems to lose his horses half the day.

The lazy mist creeps on in journey slow;
The maidens shout and wonder where they go;
So dull and dark are the November days.
The lazy mist high up the evening curled,
And now the morn quite hides in smoke and haze;
The place we occupy seems all the world.

AUTUMN EVENING

I LOVE to hear the evening crows go by
And see the starnels darken down the sky;
The bleaching stack the bustling sparrow leaves,
And plops with merry note beneath the eaves.
The odd and lated pigeon bounces by,
As if a wary watching hawk was nigh,
While far and fearing nothing, high and slow,
The stranger birds to distant places go;
While short of flight the evening robin comes
To watch the maiden sweeping out the crumbs,
Nor fears the idle shout of passing boy,
But pecks about the door, and sings for joy;
Then in the hovel where the cows are fed
Finds till the morning comes a pleasant bed.

MERRILY TO TOIL

LAPT up in sacks to shun the rain and wind,
And shoes thick-clouted with the sticking soil,
And sideling on his horse, the careless hind
Rides litherly and singing to his toil.
The boy rides foremost where the sack is gone
And holds it with his hands to keep it on;
Then splashing down the road in journey slow
Through mire and sludge with cracking whips they go.
He lays his jacket with his luncheon by
And drinks from horses' footings when adry;
They pass the maiden singing at her cow
And start the lark that roosted by the plough,
That sings above them all the livelong day
And on they drive and hollo care away.

DELUGE

THE maiden ran away to fetch the clothes
And threw her apron o'er her cap and bows;
But the shower catched her ere she hurried in
And beat and almost dowsed her to the skin.
The ruts ran brooks as they would ne'er be dry,
And the boy waded as he hurried by;
The half-drowned ploughman waded to the knees,
And birds were almost drowned upon the trees.
The streets ran rivers till they floated o'er,
And women screamed to meet it at the door.
Labour fled home and rivers hurried by,
And still it fell as it would never stop;
E'en the old stone-pit, deep as house is high,
Was brimming o'er and floated o'er the top.

WINTER WEATHER

THE crows drive onward through the storm of snow
And play about, naught caring where they go.
The young colt breaks the fences in his play
And spreads his tail and gallops all the way.
The hunkèd ploughman goes without a song
And knocks his hands and scarce can get along.
Behind the thickest hedge the labourer stands
And puts his gloves away to knock his hands.
The traveller's stooping haste to get away
Keeps both hands in his pockets all the day.
The schoolboy often stops his hands to blow
And loves to make rude letters on the snow.
While tottering shepherd, though infirm and old,
Faces the cutting wind and feels no cold.

BREAK OF DAY

THE lark he rises early,
    And the ploughman goes away
Before it's morning fairly
    At the guessing break of day;

The fields lie in the dawning,
 And the valley's hid in gold,
At the pleasant time of morning
 When the shepherd goes to fold.

The maiden laughs and hollos
 When she sees the feeding cows;
They switch their tails and follow
 When she can't get over sloughs;
I love the gentle dawning,
 And the valleys hid in gold,
At the pleasant time of morning
 When the shepherd goes to fold.

GIPSIES

THE snow falls deep; the forest lies alone;
The boy goes hasty for his load of brakes,
Then thinks upon the fire and hurries back;
The gipsy knocks his hands and tucks them up,
And seeks his squalid camp, half hid in snow,
Beneath the oak which breaks away the wind,
And bushes close in snow like hovel warm;
There tainted mutton wastes upon the coals,
And the half-wasted dog squats close and rubs,
Then feels the heat too strong, and goes aloof;
He watches well, but none a bit can spare,
And vainly waits the morsel thrown away.
'Tis thus they live—a picture to the place,
A quiet, pilfering, unprotected race.

THE MOCK BIRD

I'VE often tried, when tending sheep and cow,
With bits of grass and peels of oaten straw
To whistle like the birds. The thrush would start
To hear her song, and pause, and fly away;
The blackbird never cared but sang again;

102

The nightingale's fine song I could not try;
And when the thrush would mock her song, she paused
And sang another song no bird could do.
She sang when all were done, and beat them all.
I've often sat and mocked them half the day
Behind the hedgerow thorn or bullace tree.
I thought how nobly I could act in crowds;
The woods and fields were all the books I knew,
And every leisure thought was Love and Fame.

FIRST LOVE

No single hour can pass for naught,
    No moment-hand can move,
But calendars an aching thought
    Of my first lonely love.

Where silence doth the loudest call
    My secret to betray,
As moonlight holds the night in thrall,
    As suns reveal the day,

I hide it in the silent shades,
    Till silence finds a tongue;
I make its grave where time invades,
    Till time becomes a song.

I bid my foolish heart be still,
    But hopes will not be chid:
My heart will beat, and burn, and chill,
    First love will not be hid.

When summer ceases to be green,
    And winter bare and blea,
Death may forget what I have been
    When I shall cease to be.

When words refuse before the crowd
   My Mary's name to give,
The muse in silence sings aloud:
   And there my love will live.

WHAT IS LOVE?

SAY, what is love? To live in vain,
To live, and die, and live again?
Say, what is love? Is it to be
In prison still and still be free—
Or seem as free? Alone, and prove·
The hopeless hopes of real love?
Does real love on earth exist?
'Tis like a sunbeam in the mist,
That fades and nowhere will remain,
And nowhere is o'ertook again.
Say, what is love? A blooming name,
A rose-leaf on the page of fame,
That blooms, then fades, to cheat no more,
And is what nothing was before?
Say, what is love? Whate'er it be,
It centres, Mary, still with thee.

THE EXILE

LOVE is the mainspring of existence. It
   Becomes a soul whereby I live to love.
On all I see, that dearest name is writ;
   Falsehood is here—but truth has life above,
   Where every star that shines exists in love.
Skies vary in their clouds, the seasons vary
   From heat to cold, change cannot constant prove;
The south is bright—but smiles can act contrary;
My guide-star gilds the north, and shines with Mary.

My life hath been one love:—no, blot it out;
  My life hath been one chain of contradictions,
Madhouses, prisons, whore-shops—never doubt
  But that my life hath had some strong convictions
  That such was wrong; religion makes restrictions
I would have followed—but life turned a bubble,
  And clomb the giant stile of maledictions;
They took me from my wife, and to save trouble
I wed again, and made the error double.

Yet absence claims them both, and keeps them too,
  And locks me in a shop, in spite of law,
Among a low-lived set and dirty crew:
  Here let the Muse oblivion's curtain draw,
  And let man think—for God hath often saw
Things here too dirty for the light of day;
  For in a madhouse there exists no law.
Now stagnant grows my too refinèd clay;
I envy birds their wings to fly away.

Absence in love is worse than any fate;
  Summer is winter's desert, and the spring
Is like a ruined city desolate;
  Joy dies and hope retires on feeble wing;
  Nature sinks heedless; bird unheeded sing.
'Tis solitude in city's crowds; all move
  Like living death, though all to life still cling.
The strongest, bitterest thing that life can prove
Is woman's undisguise of hate and love.

How beautiful this hill of fern swells on,
  So beautiful the chapel peeps between
The hornbeams, with its simple bell; alone
  I wander here, hid in a palace green.
  Mary is absent, but the forest queen,
Nature, is with me; morning, noon, and gloaming,
  I write my poems in these paths unseen;
And when among these brakes and beeches roaming,
I sigh for truth and home and love and woman.

Here is the chapel yard enclosed with pales,
　　And oak-trees nearly top its little bell;
Here is the little bridge with guiding rails
　　That lead me on to many a pleasant dell;
　　The fern-owl chitters like a startled knell
To nature, yet 'tis sweet at evening still;
　　A pleasant road curves round the gentle swell,
Where nature seems to have her own sweet will,
Planting her beech and thorn about the sweet fern hill.

I have had many loves, and seek no more;
　　These solitudes my last delights shall be.
The leaf-hid forest and the lonely shore
　　Seem to my mind like beings that are free.
　　Yet would I had some eye to smile on me,
Some heart where I could make a happy home in,
　　Sweet Susan that was wont my love to be,
And Bessy of the glen—for I've been roaming
With both at morn and noon and dusky gloaming.

Cares gather round; I snap their chains in two,
　　And smile in agony and laugh in tears;
Like playing with a deadly serpent who
　　Stings to the death, there is no room for fears,
　　Where death would bring me happiness; his shears
Kill cares that hiss to poison many a vein;
　　The thought to be extinct my fate endears;
Pale death, the grand physician, cures all pain;
The dead rest well who lived for joys in vain.

This twilight seems a veil of gauze and mist;
　　Trees seem dark hills between the earth and sky;
Winds sob awake, and then a gusty hist
　　Fans through the wheat, like serpents gliding by.
　　I love to stretch my length 'tween earth and sky,
And see the inky foliage o'er me wave.
　　Though shades are still my prison where I lie,
Long use grows nature, which I easy brave,
And think how sweet cares rest within the grave.

106

Remind me not of other years, nor tell
    My broken hopes of joys they are to meet,
While thy own falsehood rings the loudest knell
    To one fond heart that aches, too cold to beat.
    Mary, how oft with fondness I repeat
That name alone to give my troubles rest;
    The very sound, though bitter, seemeth sweet;
In my love's home and thy own faithless breast,
Truth's bonds are broke and every nerve distressed.

Life is to me a dream that never wakes;
    Night finds me on this lengthening road alone;
Love is to me a thought that ever aches,
    A frost-bound thought that freezes life to stone.
    Mary, in truth and nature still my own,
That warms the winter of my aching breast,
    Thy name is joy, nor will I life bemoan;
Midnight, when sleep takes charge of nature's rest,
Finds me awake and friendless—not distressed.

Friend of the friendless, from a host of snares,
    From lying varlets and from friendly foes,
I sought thy quiet truth to ease my cares,
    And on the blight of reason found repose.
    But when the strife of nature ceased her throes,
And other hearts would beat for my return,
    I trusted fate to ease my world of woes,
Seeking love's harbour where I now sojourn;
But hell is heaven, could I cease to mourn

For her, for one whose very name is yet
    My hell or heaven, and will ever be.
Falsehood is doubt—but I can ne'er forget
    Oaths virtuous falsehood volunteered to me,
    To make my soul new bonds, which God made free.
God's gift is love, and do I wrong the giver
    To plead affections wrong from God's decree?
No, when farewell upon my lips did quiver
And all seemed lost, I loved her more than ever.

Now come the balm and breezes of the spring;
   Not with the pleasures of my early days,
When nature seemed one endless song to sing
   Of joyous melody and happy praise.
   Ah, would they come agen! But life betrays
Quicksands, and gulfs, and storms that howl and sting
   All quiet into madness and delays.
Care hides the sunshine with its raven wing,
And hell glooms sadness o'er the songs of spring.

My mind is dark and fathomless, and wears
   The hues of hopeless agony and hell;
No plummet ever sounds the soul's affairs;
   There death eternal never sounds the knell;
   There love imprisoned sighs the long farewell,
And still may sigh, in thoughts no heart hath penned,
   Alone, in loneliness where sorrows dwell;
And hopeless hope hopes on and meets no end,
Wastes without springs and homes without a friend.

Yet love lives on in every kind of weather,
   In heats and colds, in sunshine and in gloom;
Winter may blight and stormy clouds may gather,
   Nature invigorates and love will bloom;
   It fears no sorrow in a life to come,
But lives within itself from year to year,
   As doth the wild flower in its own perfume;
As in the Lapland snows spring's blooms appear,
So true love blooms and blossoms everywhere.

The dew falls on the weed and on the flower,
   The rose and thistle bathe their heads in dew;
The lowliest heart may have its prospering hour,
   The saddest bosom meets its wishes true;
   E'en I may love and happiness renew,
Though not the sweets of my first early days,
   When one sweet face was all the loves I knew,
And my soul trembled on her eyes to gaze,
Whose very censure seemed intended praise.

Flow on, my verse, though barren thou mayst be
  Of thought; yet sing, and let thy fancies roll;
In early days thou swept a mighty sea,
  All calm in troublous deeps, and spurned control.
  Thou fire and iceberg to an aching soul,
And still an angel in my gloomy way,
  Far better opiate than the draining bowl,
Still sing, my muse, to drive care's fiends away,
Nor heed what loitering listener hears the lay.

Her looks were like the spring, her very voice
  Was spring's own music, more than song to me;
Choice of my boyhood, nay, my soul's first choice,
  From her sweet thraldom I am never free.
  Yet here my prison is a spring to me,
Past memories bloom like flowers where'er I rove,
  My very bondage, though in snares, is free;
I love to stretch me in this shady grove
And muse upon the memories of love.

Hail, solitude, still peace, and lonely good,
  Thou spirit of all joys to be alone,
My best of friends, these glades and this green wood,
  Where nature is herself, and loves her own;
  The heart's hid anguish, here I make it known,
And tell my troubles to the gentle wind;
  Friends' cold neglects have froze my heart to stone,
And wrecked the voyage of a quiet mind,
With wives and friends and every hope disjoined;

Wrecked of all hopes save one, to be alone,
  Where solitude becomes my wedded mate;
Sweet forest! with rich beauties overgrown,
  Where solitude is queen and reigns in state;
  Hid in green trees, I hear the clapping gate
And voices calling to the rambling cows.
  I laugh at love and all its idle fate;
The present hour is all my lot allows;
An age of sorrow springs from lovers' vows.

109

Sweet is the song of birds, for that restores
   The soul to harmony, the mind to love;
'Tis nature's song of freedom out of doors,
   Forests beneath, free winds and clouds above;
   The thrush and nightingale and timid dove
Breathe music round me where the gipsies dwell;
   Pierced hearts, left burning in the doubts of love,
Are desolate where crowds and cities dwell;
The splendid palace seems the gates of hell.

THE RETURN: NORTHBOROUGH, 1841

Now melancholy autumn comes anew
   With showery clouds and fields of wheat tanned brown;
Along the meadow banks I peace pursue
   And see the wild flowers gleaming up and down,
   Like sun and light; the ragwort's golden crown
Mirrors like sunshine when sunbeams retire,
   And silver yarrow: there's the little town,
And o'er the meadows gleams that slender spire,
Remind me of one, and waking fond desire.

I love thee, nature, in my inmost heart;
   Go where I will, thy truth seems from above;
Go where I will, thy landscape forms a part
   Of heaven: e'en these fens, where wood nor grove
   Are seen, their very nakedness I love,
For one dwells nigh that secret hopes prefer
   Above the race of women; like the dove,
I mourn her absence; fate, that would deter
My hate for all things, strengthens love for her.

That form from boyhood loved and still loved on,
   That voice, that look, that face of one delight,
Love's register for years, months, weeks, time past and gone,
   Her looks were ne'er forgot nor out of sight.
   Mary, the muse of every song I write,
Thy cherished memory never leaves my own;
   Though care's chill winter doth my manhood blight,
And freeze, like Niobe, my thoughts to stone,
Our lives are two, our end and aim is one.

'Tis pleasant, now day's hours begin to pass
　　To dewy eve, to walk down narrow close,
And feel one's feet among refreshing grass,
　　And hear the insects in their homes discourse,
　　And startled blackbird fly, from covert close
Of whitethorn hedge, with wild fear-fluttering wings,
　　And see the spire and hear the clock toll hoarse,
And whisper names and think o'er many things
That love hurds up in truth's imaginings.

Fame blazed upon me like a comet's glare;
　　Fame waned and left me like a fallen star,
Because I told the evil what they were
　　And truth and falsehood never wished to mar;
　　My life hath been a wreck—and I've gone far
For peace and truth and hope, for home and rest;
　　Like Eden's gates, fate throws a constant bar:
Thought may o'ertake the sunset in the west,
Man meet no home within a woman's breast.

Though they are blazoned in the poet's song
　　And all the comforts which our lives contain,
I read and sought such joys my whole life long,
　　And found the best of poets sung in vain.
　　But still I read and sighed and sued again,
And lost no purpose where I had the will;
　　I almost worshipped; when my toils grew vain,
Finding no antidote my pains to kill,
I sigh, a poet and a lover still.

Dull must that being live who sees unmoved
　　The scenes and objects that his childhood knew
The schoolyard and the maid he early loved,
　　The sunny wall where long the old elms grew,
　　The grass that e'en till noon retains the dew
Beneath the walnut shade—I see them still,
　　Though not such fancies do I now pursue;
Yet still the picture turns my bosom chill,
And leaves a void nor love nor hope may fill.

111

After long absence how the mind recalls
    Pleasing associations of the past:
Haunts of his youth, thorn hedges and old walls,
    And hollow trees that sheltered from the blast,
    And all that map of boyhood, overcast
With glooms and wrongs and sorrows not his own,
    That o'er his brow like the scathed lightning past,
That turned his spring to winter, and alone
Wrecked name and fame and all, to solitude unknown.

So on he lives in glooms and living death,
    A shade like night, forgetting and forgot;
Insects, that kindle in the spring's young breath,
    Take hold of life and share a brighter lot
    Than he, the tenant of the hall and cot;
The princely palace too hath been his home,
    And gipsy's camp when friends would know him not;
In midst of wealth, a beggar still to roam,
Parted from one whose heart was once his home.

And yet not parted; still love's hope illumes,
    And like the rainbow, brightest in the storm,
It looks for joy beyond the wreck of tombs,
    And in life's winter keeps love's embers warm.
    The ocean's roughest tempest meets a calm,
Care's thickest cloud shall break in sunny joy;
    O'er the parched waste, showers yet shall fall like balm,
And she, the soul of life, for whom I sigh,
Like flowers shall cheer me when the storm is by.

SONG

THE rain is come in misty showers,
    The landscape lies in shrouds;
Patches of sunshine like to flowers
    Fall down between the clouds
And gild the earth, elsewhere so cold,
With shreds like flowers of purest gold.

And now it sweeps along the hills
    Just like a falling cloud,
The cornfields into silence stills
    Where misty moisture shrouds;
And now a darker cloud sweeps o'er,
The rain drops faster than before.

The cattle graze along the ground,
    The lark she wets her wings
And chatters as she whirls around,
    Then to the wet corn sings,
And hides upon her twitchy nest,
Refreshed, with wet and speckled breast.

And I the calm delight embrace
    To walk along the fields
And feel the rain drop in my face
    That sweetest pleasure yields;
They come from heaven and there the Free
Sends down his blessings upon me.

I love to walk in summer shower
    When the rain falls gently down,
I love to walk a leisure hour
    A distance from the town,
To see the drops on bushes hing
And blackbirds prune a dabbled wing.

A GLOOMY DAY IN SUMMER

A DULL gloom hangs above the peaceful fields,
And in one moody mist the houses sleep
Still as if tenantless. The vapour shields
The heavens like a secret that would keep
The doom sealed over our dull hours of sleep.
The evening comes as something not forgiven,
The clouds hang lowly but forbear to weep;
Noontide and evening hold the balance even,
And gloom shuts Hope's eyes from the sight of heaven.

AUTUMN

The thistledown's flying, though the winds are all still,
On the green grass now lying, now mounting the hill,
The spring from the fountain now boils like a pot;
Through stones past the counting it bubbles red-hot.

The ground parched and cracked is like overbaked bread,
The greensward all wracked is, bents dried up and dead.
The fallow fields glitter like water indeed,
And gossamers twitter, flung from weed unto weed.

Hill-tops like hot iron glitter bright in the sun,
And the rivers we're eying burn to gold as they run;
Burning hot is the ground, liquid gold is the air;
Whoever looks round sees Eternity there.

AUTUMN

I love the fitful gust that shakes
   The casement all the day,
And from the mossy elm-tree takes
   The faded leaves away,
Twirling them by the window pane
With thousand others down the lane.

I love to see the shaking twig
   Dance till the shut of eve,
The sparrow on the cottage rig,
   Whose chirp would make believe
That spring was just now flirting by
In summer's lap with flowers to lie.

I love to see the cottage smoke
   Curl upwards through the trees,
The pigeons nestled round the cote
   On November days like these;
The cock upon the dunghill crowing,
The mill-sails on the heath a-going.

The feather from the raven's breast
    Falls on the stubble lea,
The acorns near the old crow's nest
    Drop pattering down the tree;
The grunting pigs, that wait for all,
Scramble and hurry where they fall.

AUTUMN CHANGE

THE leaves of autumn drop by twos and threes,
And the black cloud hung o'er the old low church
Is fixed as is a rock that never stirs.
But look again and you may well perceive
The weathercock is in another sky,
And the cloud passing leaves the blue behind.

Crimson and yellow, blotched with iron-brown,
The autumn tans and variegates the leaves;
The nuts are ripe in woods about the town;
Russet the cleared fields where the bindweed weaves
Round stubbles and still flowers; the trefoil seeds
And troubles all the lands. From rig to furrow
There's nothing left but rubbish and foul weeds
I love to see the rabbits' snug-made burrow
Under the old hedge-bank or huge mossed oak
Claspt fast with ivy—there the rabbit breeds
Where the kite peelews and the ravens croak
And hares and rabbits at their leisure feed,
As varying autumn through her changes runs,
Season of sudden storms and brilliant suns.

THE AUTUMN WIND

THE autumn's wind on suthering wings
    Plays round the oak-tree strong
And through the hawthorn hedges sings
    The year's departing song.

There's every leaf upon the whirl
    Ten thousand times an hour,
The grassy meadows crisp and curl
    With here and there a flower.
There's nothing in this world I find
But wakens to the autumn wind.

The chaffinch flies from out the bushes,
    The bluecap 'teehees' on the tree,
The wind sues on in merry gushes
    His murmuring autumn minstrelsy.
The robin sings his autumn song
    Upon the crab-tree overhead,
The clouds of smoke they sail along,
    Leaves rustle from their mossy bed.
There's nothing suits my musing mind
Like to the pleasant autumn wind.

How many a mile it suthers on
    And stays to dally with the leaves,
And when the first broad blast is gone
    A stranger gust the foliage heaves.
The poplar-tree is turned to grey
    And crowds of leaves do by it ride,
The birch-tree dances all the day
    In concert with the rippling tide.
There's nothing calms the unquiet mind
Like to the soothing autumn's wind.

Sweet twittering o'er the meadow grass,
    Soft sueing o'er the fallow ground,
The lark starts up as on they pass
    With many a gush and moaning sound.
It fans the feathers of the bird
    And ruffles robin's ruddy breast
As round the hovel's end it swerved,
    Then sobs and sighs and goes to rest.
In solitude the musing mind
Must ever love the autumn wind.

THE SILVER MIST

THE silver mist more lowly swims
And each green-bosomed valley dims,
And o'er the neighbouring meadow lies
Like half-seen visions by dim eyes.
Green trees look grey, bright waters black,
The lated crow has lost her track
And flies by guess her journey home:
She flops along and cannot see
Her peaceful nest on oddling tree.
The lark drops down and cannot meet
The taller black-grown clumps of wheat.
The mists that rise from heat of day
Fade field and meadow all away.

MARY HELEN

THE flaggy wheat is in the ear
At the low end of the town,
And the barley horns begin to spear
The spindle through the crown;
The black snail he has crept abroad
In danger's ways to run,
And midges o'er the road
Are dancing in the sun;
When firdeals darkest shadows leave,
Sweet Mary Helen walks at eve.

In the deep dyke grows the reed,
The bulrush wabbles deeper still,
And oval leaves of waterweed
The dangerous deeper places fill;
The river winds and feels no ill.
How lovely sinks the setting sun!
The fish leaps up; with trembling trill
Grasshoppers chirrup on the reed;
The mead so green, the air so still,

117

Evening assembles sweet indeed
With Mary Helen from the hill,
Who wanders by that river's brim,
In dewy flowers and shadows dim.

Right merrily the midges dance
Above the river stream,
Their wings like silver atoms glance
In evening's golden beam;
The boat-track by the river-side,
Where Mary Helen roves,
The cloud sky where the river's wide,
The banks of yellow groves,
And Mary Helen in young pride
Rambling by the river-side.

EARLY SPRING

THE spring is come, and spring flowers coming too,
  The crocus, patty kay, the rich heartsease;
The polyanthus peeps with blebs of dew,
  And daisy flowers; the buds swell on the trees;
  While o'er the odd flowers swim grandfather bees.
In the old homestead rests the cottage cow;
  The dogs sit on their haunches near the pale,
The least one to the stranger growls 'bow-wow,'
  Then hurries to the door and cocks his tail,
To gnaw the unfinished bone; the placid cow
  Looks o'er the gate; the thresher's lumping flail
Is all the noise the spring encounters now.

ON A LANE IN SPRING

A LITTLE lane —the brook runs close beside,
  And spangles in the sunshine, while the fish glide swiftly by;
And hedges leafing with the green springtide;
  From out their greenery the old birds fly,

And chirp and whistle in the morning sun;
  The pilewort glitters 'neath the pale blue sky,
The little robin has its nest begun,
  And grass-green linnets round the bushes fly.
How mild the spring comes in! the daisy buds
  Lift up their golden blossoms to the sky.
  How lovely are the pingles and the woods!
  Here a beetle runs—and there a fly
Rests on the arum leaf in bottle-green,
And all the spring in this sweet lane is seen.

FRAGMENT

THE cataract, whirling to the precipice,
  Elbows down rocks and, shouldering, thunders through.
Roars, howls, and stifled murmurs never cease;
  Hell and its agonies seem hid below.
Thick rolls the mist, that smokes and falls in dew;
  The trees and greenwood wear the deepest green.
Horrible mysteries in the gulf stare through,
  Roars of a million tongues, and none knows what they
    mean.

DEWDROPS

THE dewdrops on every blade of grass are so much like silver drops that I am obliged to stoop down as I walk to see if they are pearls, and those sprinkled on the ivy-woven beds of primroses underneath the hazels, whitethorns, and maples are so like gold beads that I stooped down to feel if they were hard, but they melted from my finger. And where the dew lies on the primrose, the violet and whitethorn leaves, they are emerald and beryl, yet nothing more than the dews of the morning on the budding leaves; nay, the road grasses are covered with gold and silver beads, and the further we go the brighter they seem to shine, like solid gold and silver. It is nothing more than the sun's light and shade upon them in the dewy morning; every thorn-point and every bramble-spear has its tembling ornament: till the wind gets a little brisker, and then all is shaken off, and all the shining jewelry passes away into a common spring morning full of budding leaves, primroses, violets, vernal speedwell, bluebell and orchis, and commonplace objects.

HOUSE OR WINDOW FLIES

THESE little indoor dwellers, in cottages and halls, were always entertaining to me; after dancing in the window all day from sunrise to sunset they would sip of the tea, drink of the beer, and eat of the sugar, and be welcome all summer long. They look like things of mind or fairies, and seem pleased or dull as the weather permits. In many clean cottages and genteel houses, they are allowed every liberty to creep, fly, or do as they like; and seldom or ever do wrong. In fact they are the small or dwarfish portion of our own family, and so many fairy familiars that we know and treat as one of ourselves.

PLEASANT SOUNDS

THE rustling of leaves under the feet in woods and under hedges;

The crumping of cat-ice and snow down wood-rides, narrow lanes, and every street causeway;

Rustling through a wood or rather rushing, while the wind halloos in the oak-top like thunder;

The rustle of birds' wings startled from their nests or flying unseen into the bushes;

The whizzing of larger birds overhead in a wood, such as crows, puddocks, buzzards;

The trample of robins and woodlarks on the brown leaves, and the patter of squirrels on the green moss;

The fall of an acorn on the ground, the pattering of nuts on the hazel branches as they fall from ripeness;

The flirt of the groundlark's wing from the stubbles—how sweet such pictures on dewy mornings, when the dew flashes from its brown feathers!

THE TELL-TALE FLOWERS

AND has the spring's all-glorious eye
   No lesson to the mind?
The birds that cleave the golden sky,
   Things to the earth resigned,
Wild flowers that dance to every wind—
Do they no memory leave behind?

Ay, flowers! The very name of flowers,
   That bloom in wood and glen,
Brings spring to me in winter's hours,
   And childhood's dreams agen.
The primrose on the woodland lea
Was more than gold and lands to me.

The violets by the woodland side
   Are thick as they could thrive;
I've talked to them with childish pride
   As things that were alive:
I find them now in my distress—
They seem as sweet, yet valueless.

The cowslips on the meadow lea,
   How have I run for them!
I looked with wild and childish glee
   Upon each golden gem:
And when they bowed their heads so shy
I laughed, and thought they danced for joy

And when a man, in early years,
   How sweet they used to come,
And give me tales of smiles and tears,
   And thoughts more dear than home:
Secrets which words would then reprove
They told the names of early love.

The primrose turned a babbling flower
   Within its sweet recess;
I blushed to see its secret bower,
   And turned her name to bless.
The violets said the eyes were blue
I loved, and did they tell me true?

The cowslips, blooming everywhere,
　My heart's own thoughts could steal;
I nipt them that they should not hear:
　They smiled, and would reveal;
And o'er each meadow, right or wrong,
They sing the name I've worshipped long.

The brook that mirrored clear the sky—
　Full well I know the spot;
The mouse-ear looked with bright blue eye,
　And said, 'Forget me not.'
And from the brook I turned away,
But heard it many an after day.

The kingcup on its slender stalk,
　Within the pasture dell,
Would picture there a pleasant walk
　With one I loved so well.
It said, 'How sweet at eventide
'Twould be, with true love at thy side.'

And on the pasture's woody knoll
　I saw the wild bluebell,
On Sundays where I used to stroll
　With her I loved so well:
She culled the flowers the year before;
These bowed, and told the story o'er.

And every flower that had a name
　Would tell me who was fair;
But those without, as strangers, came
　And blossomed silent there:
I stood to hear, but all alone
They bloomed and kept their thoughts unknown.

But seasons now have naught to say,
　The flowers no news to bring:
Alone I live from day to day—
　Flowers deck the bier of spring;
And birds upon the bush or tree
All sing a different tale to me.

THE MAPLE-TREE

THE maple with its tassel flowers of green,
That turns to red a staghorn-shapèd seed,
Just spreading out its scolloped leaves is seen,
Of yellowish hue, yet beautifully green;
Bark ribbed like corduroy in seamy screed,
That farther up the stem is smoother seen,
Where the white hemlock with white umbel flowers
Up each spread stoven to the branches towers;
And moss around the stoven spreads, dark green,
And blotched-leaved orchis, and the bluebell flowers:
Thickly they grow and 'neath the leaves are seen;
I love to see them gemmed with morning hours,
I love the lone green places where they be,
And the sweet clothing of the maple-tree.

LITTLE TROTTY WAGTAIL

LITTLE trotty wagtail, he went in the rain,
And tittering, tottering sideways he ne'er got straight again,
He stooped to get a worm, and looked up to catch a fly,
And then he flew away ere his feathers they were dry.

Little trotty wagtail, he waddled in the mud,
And left his little footmarks, trample where he would.
He waddled in the water-pudge, and waggle went his tail,
And chirrup up his wings to dry upon the garden rail.

Little trotty wagtail, you nimble all about,
And in the dimpling water-pudge you waddle in and out;
Your home is nigh at hand, and in the warm pigsty,
So, little Master Wagtail, I'll bid you a good-bye.

CLOCK-A-CLAY

In the cowslip pips I lie,
Hidden from the buzzing fly,
While green grass beneath me lies,
Pearled with dew like fishes' eyes,
Here I lie, a clock-a-clay,
Waiting for the time of day.

While grassy forest quakes surprise,
And the wild wind sobs and sighs,
My gold home rocks as like to fall,
On its pillar green and tall;
When the pattering rain drives by
Clock-a-clay keeps warm and dry.

Day by day and night by night,
All the week I hide from sight;
In the cowslip pips I lie,
In rain and dew still warm and dry;
Day and night, and night and day,
Red, black-spotted clock-a-clay.

My home shakes in wind and showers,
Pale green pillar topped with flowers,
Bending at the wild wind's breath,
Till I touch the grass beneath;
Here I live, lone clock-a-clay,
Watching for the time of day.

THE PAST

THE present is the funeral of the past,
And man the living sepulchre of life.
Still in the past he lives—oh, would it last
In its own dreams of beauty, where the strife
Of passion died! Yet trouble ever rife
Dwells on its sweetest tones, and harsh all sound.
That chord that used to sound the name of wife
On life's jarred music now emits no sound,
And sweetheart melodies lost are nowhere to be found.

THE DYING CHILD

HE could not die when trees were green,
   For he loved the time too well.
His little hands, when flowers were seen,
   Were held for the bluebell,
      As he was carried o'er the green.

His eye glanced at the white-nosed bee;
  He knew those children of the spring:
When he was well and on the lea
  He held one in his hands to sing,
    Which filled his heart with glee.

Infants, the children of the spring!
  How can an infant die
When butterflies are on the wing,
  Green grass, and such a sky?
    How can they die at spring?

He held his hands for daisies white,
  And then for violets blue,
And took them all to bed at night
  That in the green fields grew,
    As childhood's sweet delight.

And then he shut his little eyes,
  And flowers would notice not;
Birds' nests and eggs caused no surprise,
  He now no blossoms got:
    They met with plaintive sighs.

When winter came and blasts did sigh,
  And bare were plain and tree,
As he for ease in bed did lie
  His soul seemed with the free,
    He died so quietly.

MY SCHOOLBOY DAYS

THE spring is come forth, but no spring is for me
Like the spring of my boyhood on woodland and lea,
When flowers brought me heaven and knew me again,
In the joy of their blooming o'er mountain and plain.
My thoughts are confined and imprisoned: oh, when
Will freedom find me my own valleys agen?

The wind breathes so sweet, and the day is so calm;
In the woods and the thicket the flowers look so warm;
And the grass is so green, so delicious and sweet;
Oh, when shall my manhood my youth's valleys meet—
The scenes where my children are laughing at play—
The scenes that from memory are fading away?

The primrose looks happy in every field;
In strange woods the violets their odours will yield,
And flowers in the sunshine, all brightly arrayed,
Will bloom just as fresh and as sweet in the shade,
But the wild flowers that bring me most joy and content
Are the blossoms that glow where my childhood was spent.

The trees are all naked, the bushes are bare,
And the fields are as brown as if winter was there;
But the violets are there by the dykes and the dell,
Where I played 'hen and chickens' and heard the church bell
Which called me to prayer-book and sermons in vain:
Oh, when shall I see my own valleys again?

There the churches look bright as sun at noon-day;
There the meadows look green ere the winter's away;
There the pooty still lies for the schoolboy to find,
And a thought often brings these sweet places to mind;
Where trees waved and wind moaned; no music so well:
There naught sounded harsh but the school-calling bell.

There are spots where I played, there are spots where I loved,
There are scenes where the tales of my choice were approved,
As green as at first, and their memory will be
The dearest of life's recollections to me.
The objects seen there, in the care of my heart,
Are as fair as at first, and will never depart.

Though no names are mentioned to sanction my themes,
Their hearts beat with mine, and make real my dreams;
Their memories with mine their diurnal course run,
True as night to the stars and as day to the sun;
And as they are now, so their memories will be,
While sense, truth, and reason remain here with me.

MY EARLY HOME

HERE sparrows build upon the trees,
  And stock-dove hides her nest;
The leaves are winnowed by the breeze
  Into a calmer rest;
The blackcap's song was very sweet,
  That used the rose to kiss;
It made the paradise complete:
  My early home was this.

The redbreast from the sweetbrier bush
  Dropt down to pick the worm;
On the horse-chestnut sang the thrush,
  O'er the house where I was born;
The moonlight, like a shower of pearls,
  Fell o'er this 'bower of bliss,'
And on the bench sat boys and girls:
  My early home was this.

The old house stooped just like a cave,
  Thatched o'er with mosses green;
Winter around the walls would rave,
  But all was calm within;
The trees are here all green agen,
  Here bees the flowers still kiss,
But flowers and trees seemed sweeter then:
  My early home was this.

NOW IS PAST

Now is past—the happy *now*
  When we together roved
Beneath the wildwood's oak-tree bough
  And nature said we loved.
      Winter's blast.
The *now* since then has crept between,
  And left us both apart.
Winters that withered all the green
  Have froze the beating heart.
      Now is past.

Now is past since last we met
    Beneath the hazel bough;
Before the evening sun was set
    Her shadow stretched below.
        Autumn's blast
Has stained and blighted every bough;
    Wild strawberries like her lips
Have left the mosses green below,
    Her bloom's upon the hips.
        Now is past.

Now is past, is changed agen,
    The woods and fields are painted new.
Wild strawberries which both gathered then,
    None know now where they grew.
        The sky's o'ercast.
Wood strawberries faded from wood-sides,
    Green leaves have all turned yellow;
No Adelaide walks the wood-rides,
    True love has no bed-fellow.
        Now is past.

FIRST LOVE

I NE'ER was struck before that hour
    With love so sudden and so sweet.
Her face it bloomed like a sweet flower
    And stole my heart away complete.
My face turned pale as deadly pale,
    My legs refused to walk away,
And when she looked 'what could I ail?'
    My life and all seemed turned to clay.

And then my blood rushed to my face
    And took my sight away.
The trees and bushes round the place
    Seemed midnight at noonday.
I could not see a single thing,
    Words from my eyes did start;
They spoke as chords do from the string
    And blood burnt round my heart.

Are flowers the winter's choice?
  Is love's bed always snow?
She seemed to hear my silent voice
  And love's appeal to know.
I never saw so sweet a face
  As that I stood before:
My heart has left its dwelling-place
  And can return no more.

HOW CAN I FORGET?

THAT farewell voice of love is never heard again,
Yet I remember it, and think on it with pain;
I see the place she spoke when passing by,
The flowers were blooming as her form drew nigh;
That voice is gone with every pleasing tone,
Loved but one moment, and the next alone.

'Farewell!' the woods repeated as she went
Walking in silence through the grassy bent;
The wild flowers, they ne'er looked so sweet before,
Bowed in farewells to her they'll see no more.
In this same spot the wild flowers bloom the same
In scent and hue and shape, ay, even name;
'Twas here she said farewell, and no one yet
Has so sweet spoken.   How can I forget?

SECRET LOVE

I HID my love when young till I
Couldn't bear the buzzing of a fly;
I hid my love to my despite
Till I could not bear to look at light
I dare not gaze upon her face
But left her memory in each place
Where'er I saw a wild flower lie
I kissed and bade my love good-bye.

I met her in the greenest dells,
Where dewdrops pearl the wood bluebells;
The lost breeze kissed her bright blue eye,
The bee kissed and went singing by,
A sunbeam found a passage there,
A gold chain round her neck so fair;
As secret as the wild bee's song
She lay there all the summer long.

I hid my love in field and town
Till e'en the breeze would knock me down;
The bees seemed singing ballads o'er,
The fly's bass turned a lion's roar;
And even silence found a tongue,
To haunt me all the summer long;
The riddle nature could not prove
Was nothing else but secret love.

INVITATION TO ETERNITY

SAY, wilt thou go with me, sweet maid,
Say, maiden, wilt thou go with me
Through the valley-depths of shade,
Of night and dark obscurity;
Where the path has lost its way,
Where the sun forgets the day,
Where there's nor light nor life to see,
Sweet maiden, wilt thou go with me?

Where stones will turn to flooding streams,
Where plains will rise like ocean's waves,
Where life will fade like visioned dreams
And mountains darken into caves,
Say, maiden, wilt thou go with me
Through this sad non-identity,
Where parents live and are forgot,
And sisters live and know us not?

Say, maiden, wilt thou go with me
In this strange death-in-life to be,
To live in death and be the same,
Without this life or home or name,
At once to be and not to be—
That was and is not—yet to see
Things pass like shadows, and the sky
Above, below, around us lie?

The land of shadows wilt thou trace,
Nor look nor know each other's face;
The present marred with reason gone,
And past and present all as one?
Say, maiden, can thy life be led
To join the living and the dead?
Then trace thy footsteps on with me;
We are wed to one eternity.

POETS LOVE NATURE

Poets love nature, and themselves are love,
Though scorn of fools, and mock of idle pride.
The vile in nature worthless deeds approve,
They court the vile and spurn all good beside.
Poets love nature; like the calm of heaven,
Like heaven's own love, her gifts spread far and wide:
In all her works there are no signs of leaven;
Sorrow abashes from her simple pride.
Her flowers, like pleasures, have their season's birth,
They are her very scriptures upon earth,
And teach us simple mirth where'er we go.
Even in prison they can solace me,
For where they bloom God is, and I am free.

TO JOHN CLARE

Well, honest John, how fare you now at home?
The spring is come, and birds are building nests
The old cock-robin to the sty is come.
With olive feathers and its ruddy breast;

And the old cock, with wattles and red comb,
Struts with the hens, and seems to like some best,
Then crows, and looks about for little crumbs,
Swept out by little folks an hour ago;
The pigs sleep in the sty; the bookman comes—
The little boy lets home-close nesting go,
And pockets tops and taws, where daisies blow,
To look at the new number just laid down,
With lots of pictures, and good stories too,
And Jack the Giant-killer's high renown.

WRITTEN IN PRISON

I ENVY e'en the fly its gleams of joy
In the green woods; from being but a boy
Among the vulgar and the lowly bred,
I envied e'en the hare her grassy bed.
Inured to strife and hardships from a child,
I traced with lonely step the desert wild;
Sighed o'er bird pleasures, but no nest destroyed;
With pleasure felt the singing they enjoyed;
Saw nature smile on all and shed no tears,
A slave through ages, though a child in years;
The mockery and scorn of those more old,
An Aesop in the world's extended fold.
The fly I envy settling in the sun
On the green leaf, and wish my rest was won.

I AM

I AM: yet what I am none cares or knows,
    My friends forsake me like a memory lost;
I am the self-consumer of my woes,
    They rise and vanish in oblivious host,
Like shades in love and death's oblivion lost;
And yet I am, and live with shadows tost

Into the nothingness of scorn and noise,
    Into the living sea of waking dreams,

Where there is neither sense of life nor joys,
    But the vast shipwreck of my life's esteems;
And e'en the dearest—that I loved the best—
Are strange—nay, rather stranger than the rest.

I long for scenes where man has never trod,
    A place where woman never smiled or wept;
There to abide with my Creator, God,
    And sleep as I in childhood sweetly slept:
Untroubling and untroubled where I lie,
The grass below—above the vaulted sky.

THE SLEEP OF SPRING

Oh, for that sweet, untroubled rest
    That poets oft have sung!—
The babe upon its mother's breast,
    The bird upon its young,
The heart asleep without a pain—
When shall I know that sleep again?

When shall I be as I have been
    Upon my mother's breast
Sweet nature's garb of verdant green
    To woo to perfect rest—
Love in the meadow, field, and glen
And in my native wilds agen?

The sheep within the fallow field,
    The herd upon the green,
The larks that in the thistle shield,
    And pipe from morn to e'en—
Oh for the pasture, field, and fen!
When shall I see such rest agen?

I love the weeds along the fen,
    More sweet than garden flowers,
For freedom haunts the humble glen
    That blest my happiest hours.
Here prison injures health and me:
I love sweet freedom and the free.

The crows upon the swelling hills,
    The cows upon the lea,
Sheep feeding by the pasture rills,
    Are ever dear to me,
Because sweet freedom is their mate
While I am lone and desolate.

I loved the winds when I was young,
    When life was dear to me;
I loved the song which nature sung,
    Endearing liberty;
I loved the wood, the vale, the stream,
For there my boyhood used to dream.

There even toil itself was play;
    'Twas pleasure e'en to weep;
'Twas joy to think of dreams by day,
    The beautiful of sleep.
When shall I see the wood and plain,
And dream those happy dreams again?

I LOST THE LOVE OF HEAVEN

I LOST the love of heaven above,
    I spurned the lust of earth below,
I felt the sweets of fancied love,
    And hell itself my only foe.

I lost earth's joys, but felt the glow
    Of heaven's flame about in me,
Till loveliness and I did grow
    The bard of immortality.

I loved, but woman fell away;
    I hid me from her faded flame.
I snatched the sun's eternal ray
    And wrote till earth was but a name.

In every language upon earth,
    On every shore, o'er every sea,
I gave my name immortal birth
    And kept my spirit with the free.

GLOSSARY OF DIALECT WORDS

agen: against, near

bandy: a game like hockey
baulk: narrow strip of grassland dividing open ploughed fields
beaking: basking
bevering: (adj.) refreshment
blea: bleak, exposed
bluecap: blue tit
brig: bridge
brustling: rustling
bullace: variety of sloe
bum: to buzz

chickering: chirping of cricket
chitter: to chatter, twitter, rustle
chock: game with marbles
chuffy: fat
clack: chatter
clammed: parched
clock-a-clay: ladybird
clouted: patched, repaired
clumpsing: benumbed
copple: crest on bird's head
copt: (of hay) put into heaps
corn-bottle: cornflower
crankle: to twist sinuously
craw: crop of a bird
crimp: to ripple, wrinkle
crimple: to ripple, ruffle
crump: to crackle
cuckaball: ball of flowers for throwing in May games
culverkey: vetch
curdle: ripple, to twist or curl

daggled: dirtied by mud
dimp: to dimple
dither: to shiver with cold
dotterel: pollard tree
dowse: to drench
drabble: to trail in the mud
dropple: drop
drowk: to droop
ducking-stone: game of knocking stones off a pile

elting: (of soil new ploughed) moist

fern-owl: nightjar
firdeal: fir-tree
fother: to fodder
freak: to mark with spots, dapple
frit: frightened

glib: (of ice) smooth, slippery
goss: gorse

hapt: covered up
hing: to hang
hist: hissing noise
hunked: dispirited
hurd: to hoard
hurkle: to crouch
hush: (adj.) silent

keck: dried stalk of hemlock or similar plant
knap: to crop
knarl: to gnaw, nibble

135

lady-cow: ladybird
lambtoe: bird's-foot trefoil
lap: to wrap
litherly: lazily
lump: to thump, thresh

maul: to drag
mizzled: misted over
moping: vacant
mort: a great number
mouldiwarp: mole

nimble: to move quickly

oddling: solitary

peep: single blossom of flowers growing in cluster
perk: jaunty
pettichap: chiff-chaff, willow warbler
pingle: clump of trees
pismire: ant
plashy: wet, splashy
pleachy: sun-dried, bleached
pooty: girdled snail shell
prog: to prod
prune: to preen
puddock: buzzard, kite
pudge: puddle

quirk: to search
quirking: nimble

ramp: to grow luxuriantly
reasty: rancid
rig: ridge of building or land

sawn: to saunter
screed: long strip of material
seethe: to soak
sideling: sideways
sile: to glide
sluther: to slide

soodle: to linger, saunter
spindle: to shoot up rapidly shoot or stem of plant
sprent: to sprinkle
sputter: to run quickly
squash: to splash
starnel: starling
stoven: stump of tree
strime: to stride
struttle: any small freshwater fish
stubs: stubble
stulp: stump of tree
sturt: to move suddenly, start
sue: to sough
suther: to make a rushing sound
suthering: noise of wind in trees
swale, swail: shade, shady place
swaly: shady
swee: to swing, a swing
swoof: sigh, grief
swop: to swoop

taw: marble
tedded: (of grass) spread out to dry
totter grass: quaking grass
tray: feeding-trough, large hurdle
twitch: spear grass, couch grass

unbrunt: unscathed

water-blob: marsh marigold
whew: to whirl, rush through the air
whimble: boring tool
woodchat: wood warbler
wood-seer: white froth made by larvae of frog-hopper
wracked: ruined

yoe: ewe
younker: youngster

INDEX OF TITLES

INDEX OF FIRST LINES